McGRAW-HILL READING

Language Support

Teacher's Manual

Grade 5 Lessons/Practice/Blackline Masters

Macmillan McGraw-Hill

New York   Farmington

Table of Contents

Grade 5

Unit 3

Unit 4

Unit 5

Unit 6

INTRODUCTION

As a dynamic social process, learning calls for students and teachers to be partners. This Language Support Manual, which accompanies MCGRAW-HILL READING, was developed to help you achieve that partnership.

Throughout this Language Support Manual you will find strategies and activities designed to help ESL students become participants in classroom learning communities with their English-speaking peers. Based on current and proven methods for teaching ESL students, these strategies and activities reflect important ideas about the learner's role and about language and communication, which are at the heart of MCGRAW-HILL READING.

For ease of reference, this introduction is divided into two parts: the first part, **Teaching the ESL Student**, is designed to orient you to the unique needs of the ESL learner; and the second part, **Teaching the Reading Selection**, mirrors the corresponding lesson in the Teacher's Edition and offers suggestions on how to present the reading skills and concepts for classes with native speakers and second language students.

Students and teachers are partners in learning.

Sheltered Instruction

Teaching the ESL Student

This section of the introduction will help you adapt your skills to meet the needs of the ESL student. Differences between teaching native English speakers and ESL students are linguistic, social, and cultural. It is not enough for ESL students to know the appropriate language to use in a given context, although this is certainly critical. In addition, you, as teacher, must ensure that ESL students are active and equal participants in the classroom. Students must be made to feel that their contributions are valuable even though they may only approximate native English speaker accuracy. They must also feel that their culture and prior experience have a respected place in the classroom.

In the following chart, we provide you with the characteristics of language learners in each of the four stages of second language acquisition. You will find it useful in identifying language behavior and building a profile of your ESL students. In the remainder of this section, we will outline procedures and activities for accommodating ESL students, strategies for meeting their unique needs, group interaction patterns that foster effective learning, the classroom environment, assessment tools, and social factors and their relevance to learning.

Stages of Second-Language Acquisition

Like their English-speaking classmates, ESL students will be at different levels of language and literacy proficiency in their native language. They will also be in various stages of English language acquisition. This Language Support Manual lists teaching prompts at four different levels which follow the chart below and summarizes the four stages of second language acquisition. As your ESL students move through the four stages, this chart may be helpful in making informal assessments of their language ability and in determining which prompts you should use.

Preproduction

nonverbal prompt for active participation

- Teachers ask students to communicate with gestures, actions, yes/no answers, and names.
- Lessons focus on listening comprehension.
- Lessons build receptive vocabulary.

(Reading and writing are incorporated.)

Early Production

one- or two- word response prompt

- Teachers ask students to respond to *either/or* questions.
- Students respond with one or two word phrases.
- Lessons expand receptive vocabulary.
- Activities encourage students to produce vocabulary they already understand.

(Reading and writing are incorporated.)

Speech Emergence

prompt for short answers to higher-level thinking skills

- Students respond in longer phrases or sentences.
- Teachers model correct language forms.
- Lessons continue to develop receptive vocabulary.

(Reading and writing are incorporated.)

Intermediate Fluency

prompt for detailed answers to higher-level thinking skills

- Students engage in conversation and produce connected narrative.
- Teachers model correct language forms.
- Reading and writing are incorporated.

Procedures and Activities

The teacher's role in the scaffolding process is to provide necessary and meaningful support toward each learning objective. The scaffolding process requires the student to take ownership for learning and the teacher to provide appropriate direction and support in teaching. It requires a form of collaboration between teachers and students in which both work together to ensure that students internalize rules and strategies for meaning-making. The following components of sheltered language instruction are methods which support the needs of second language learners and provide for optimal language arts learning.

- Reciprocal Teaching
- Cooperative Grouping
- Cross-age Tutoring

Reciprocal Teaching

Reciprocal teaching is one way to help ESL students successfully complete academic tasks. The process of reciprocal teaching involves structuring an interaction, assessing the student's comprehension from the response, and then restructuring the interaction to clarify or correct the student's response. As with other kinds of interactions in the classroom, *reciprocal teaching should be modeled and practiced as a whole class first, then it should be practiced in pairs.* The following are just some of the benefits which occur when this approach is implemented in the classroom.

- Teachers can show students not only what to learn but how to learn.
- Group interaction lends itself to varied learning styles.
- Students accept new responsibilities through a cooperative approach.
- Students' self-esteem is enhanced through shared responsibilities.
- Collaborative learning yields greater motivation, particularly for students at risk.

Cooperative Grouping

Through cooperative grouping, which is also very collaborative, students gradually assume responsibility for their learning. This approach is most effective when there is individual accountability. *Cooperative learning best provides the non-native speaker with opportunities similar to social experiences within which the native speakers have acquired the language.*

Cross-age Tutoring

The cross-age tutoring format provides yet another opportunity for students to study and learn together. *ESL students benefit from cross-age tutoring as they are engaged in focused conversation that will support their second language development.* Cross-age or peer tutoring has also been found to promote positive reading attitudes and habits.

Reciprocal teaching, cooperative grouping, and cross-age tutoring are approaches within the pedagogical framework of sheltered English instruction. The benefit of these varied grouping formats is that group members become interested in each other's opinions, feelings and interests. ESL students begin to feel more comfortable expressing themselves on the topic or in the presentation.

Successful Group Interaction

How do I insure that ESL students participate?

nonverbal prompt for active participation

Being sensitive to the cultural backgrounds of ESL students is a critical function of the teacher. In many cultures, the teacher has absolute authority in the classroom and students play a relatively passive role. Students from such cultures may not participate as vigorously as their classmates.

Elicit experiences that relate to students' native cultures.

By creating a safe environment both in the classroom, and within the group structure, students will begin to participate more freely. You may facilitate this by eliciting experiences and including activities that relate to students' native cultures. For example, if you are discussing the weather, have students talk about the weather in their countries and ask them to bring in pictures that show the range of weather in their country. Ask such questions as: *Draw a picture of a rainy and cloudy day in your country.* This Language Support Manual offers many opportunities to incorporate individual cultural backgrounds. Every lesson includes activity suggestions and teaching prompts which introduce skills and strategies through a compare/contrast matrix in the **Evaluate Prior Knowledge** and **Develop Oral Language** sections.

How should I group my native English students and ESL students for maximum learning and cooperation?

ESL students benefit from social interactions with native speakers.

Social interaction plays an important role in language development. In group work, ESL students benefit from interactions with native speakers by having more chances to try out the language they are learning. But effective group work depends on careful organization, thoughtful selection of groups, and the active involvement of the teacher.

Additionally, the following chart details various strategies that can enhance both reading comprehension as well as the oral language proficiency of second language learners.

Modeling

How do I adapt my teaching methods to accommodate the ESL learner?

Illustrate the Concept

In addition to traditional board work, ESL students need a significant amount more support and practice than native English speakers. Therefore it is essential that you give those students the necessary practice and it is vital that this support comes in the form of experiential and oral activities, before written work or reading. For example, writing the words *big* and *small* on the board and then asking students to name objects in either category, is not an adequate presentation for ESL learners. A more successful technique would be to illustrate the concepts through the use of physical objects in the room. For example, taking words that have already been associated with their objects, the teacher points to the larger of the two and says *This is big.* The students then repeat the phrase after the teacher's model. Next, the teacher points to the smaller object and says This is small. The students respond as

A Pedagogical Overview of Strategic Sheltered Instruction

SCAFFOLD	APPROPRIATE TASKS	BENEFIT TO THE READER
Modeling	Teacher models task and provides examples. Individual/Group oral reading, repetitions. Direct experience through practice.	Clarifies concepts Provides understanding of objective
Connecting Content	Questions in: Think-Pair-Share Three-Step Interview Quick-Writes Anticipatory Charts Brainstorming	Addresses students' prior knowledge Provides a personal connection between learner and theme of the class.
Creating a Context	Visualizations Focus questions and: Use of manipulatives Self-involvement Instructor provides an experiential environment. Students demonstrate knowledge for authentic audiences.	Enhances context and concept familiarity
Bridging Concepts	Compare/Contrast Matrix used as advanced organizer Story Graph used to skim through a text	Students gain heightened insight of the varied uses of the language. Students develop connections between concepts.
Perceptual Understanding	Reciprocal Teaching Self-monitoring Self-assessment Students discuss and model reading strategies	Self-autonomy is fostered Enhances students' knowledge of strategies through a conscious focus on the processes
Extension	Drama Journal writing Story Boards Post cards/letters Collaborative posters with text Eye-witness accounts	Students extend their understandings and personal relevance as they apply information to novel formats.

in the previous example. The teacher can then point to two other objects (or pictures), one big and one small. Given the teacher's cue, the students point to and classify the two objects as either big or small.

By assisting the learner in producing utterances beyond his or her capacity, you are providing 'scaffolding'—that is, the necessary support and guidance needed for the learner's growth. Through this collaboration of teacher and student, the student should progress towards greater autonomy and ownership of his or her language, thereby fostering greater self-esteem and independence.

Total Physical Response

What activities should I use to supplement teaching?

ESL students need to cover concepts using a variety of sensory input. Total Physical Response (TPR) is a well-established and successful technique that links language to a physical response. The classic game of "Simon Says" is a vivid example. The teacher (or a student) can call out a series of

Suggested TPR Commands

Stand up	Giggle	Turn your head to the *right*
Sit down	Make a face	Drum your fingers
Touch the *floor*	Flex your muscles	Wet your lips
Raise your *arm*	Wave to *me*	Blow a kiss
Put down your *arm*	Shrug your shoulders	Cough
Pat your *cheek*	Tickle your *side*	Sneeze
Wipe your *face*	Clap your hands	Shout *your name* ("help")
Scratch your *knee*	Point to the *ceiling*	Spell *your name*
Massage your *neck*	Cry	Laugh
Stretch	Yawn	Sing
Whisper *(a word)*	Hum	Hop on *one foot*
Step *forward*	Lean *backwards*	Make a fist
Shake your *hand*	(Name), walk to the door	(Name), turn on the *lights.*

Source: Richard-Amato, P. (1996) Making it happen: *Interaction in the second-language classroom,* 2nd ed. White Plains, N.Y.: Addison-Wesley Publishing Group/Longman.

commands (i.e., "Simon says, touch your toes,") and students respond with the appropriate physical gesture—in this case, by touching their toes. The advantage of this technique is it links language to the "here and now," giving learners, especially at the early stages, a concrete forum for language practice.

Because of linguistic, social, and cultural differences, ESL students will probably not cover concepts as quickly as native English speaking students. The teacher must be patient with these students and give them extra activities with varied sensory input. As with all learners, varying the pace and type of sensory input is essential—both for accommodating the various learning style preferences and maintaining interest in the lesson.

Connecting Content

How do I know my ESL students understand me?

Don't assume that ESL students don't know the answer.

When you question your students and get no answer don't automatically conclude that students don't know the answer. Adapt your questioning strategies to help ESL students understand what you say. Rephrase the question. Replace difficult vocabulary with words students know. Add context by using pictures, objects, graphic organizers to support meaning. Use gestures and facial expressions to cue feelings and moods. Draw analogies to past experiences.

Creating A Context

The Language Support Manual includes several blackline masters which coincide with the skills and strategies being taught within a reading selection. The blackline masters provide manipulatives to help students explore and practice skills. Use of manipulatives helps to enhance context while building concept familiarity.

Use of Manipulatives

How do I set up the classroom as a strategic learning environment?

The environment of the classroom can have a great impact on students' ability to learn. The following are some ways to make the classroom environment more comfortable so that ESL students can get as much as possible out of their classroom experiences.

The Classroom Environment

Create areas in the room designed to give ESL students opportunities to use the target language. For instance, if you are teaching the names of fruits, set up a "fruit market" and have students ask the "shopkeeper" for the fruits they want to buy. They can talk about how the fruits look and taste, how to prepare them, and how much they cost.

Special areas in the room provide chances for students to apply their English skills.

Set up a learner library with favorite books the students have chosen. Provide a "discussion" area where ESL students may sit with native language speakers to discuss their favorite books or to read to each other. Seating arrangements should always provide for flexible grouping.

Bridging Concepts

How do I activate 'prior knowledge' for students from a different culture?

Allow ESL students to make connections for themselves.

With native English speaking students, the teacher has common ground on which to activate the students' prior knowledge. Although American culture is very diverse, there are certain associations and symbols that are familiar to all those who live here. However, for the ESL student the teacher faces a difficult challenge—being able to activate the students' prior knowledge often without knowledge of the students' cultures. With ESL students, as with all students, the teacher should be sure to allow students to make connections for themselves. Often the teacher has a pre-determined idea of the connection and by imposing that notion on the student, he or she does not serve the students' needs to the fullest. It is important for ESL students to develop autonomy and self-esteem.

Assessment

Use alternative ways to assess ESL students' learning.

How do I assess ESL learners?

When assessing ESL students' learning, you need to adapt your expectations of what constitutes an appropriate response. Assessment that relies heavily on a written test or questionnaire, on written answers or an essay, or on answering oral questions verbally, may present problems for ESL students. Some alternative strategies include the following:

Invite students to draw, show, or point to objects.

• Allow students to draw, show, or point to an object, a procedure, or an illustration, rather than write or talk about it.

Your observations may serve as a form of assessment.

• Use your own observations and interactions with the students as a basis for assessment.

Students may perform activities to demonstrate their understanding.

• Ask students to perform an activity that will show the application of a concept. For instance, say: *Show me how a tired person acts.*

Teaching the Reading Selection to Students Needing Language Support

Each Language Support lesson in this Language Support Teacher's Guide mirrors the corresponding lesson in the Teacher's Edition of McGraw-Hill Reading. It either builds directly on that lesson, offering suggestions on how to adapt materials for students needing additional language support, or it offers alternative teaching and activities. The blackline masters following each lesson provide tools for students to use with alternative activities that develop skills and strategies taught in the lesson.

In this overview, the Language Support lesson described is from the grade one unit theme, Stories to Tell. The selection, *Sam's Song,* is the story of a young owl who learns to sing with her family. Variations on the lesson in Grades K, 3-6 are noted where appropriate.

Focus on Reading

Develop Phonological Awareness (Grades K-2)

Help develop children's awareness of sounds.

This part of the Language Support lesson is designed to help children develop their ability to hear the sounds in spoken language. These skills can be improved through systematic, explicit instruction involving auditory practice. Each selection in grades K-2 begins with a lesson designed to focus the children's attention on a particular phonological skill. In the grade one selection, for example, children are asked to listen for digraphs, *ch, wh,* and *nk.* As you read aloud the poem, "Lunch Munch," children are asked to clap their hands each time they hear a word that rhyme with *bunch.* The activity is repeated with the word *think.*

Children who may be having difficulty hearing these sounds are guided through an activity in which they make up a series of tongue twisters containing the digraphs. For example: *The child chomps on a chip.* Students listen for and identify the words in which they hear /ch/.

In these practical, learner-centered lessons from the Language Support Teacher's Guide, children are often asked to respond physically to the sounds they hear. For example, in this grade one lesson, they are asked to whistle, chomp, or blink when they hear words with *wh, ch,* or *nk.*

The Language Support Teacher's Manual identifies these activities as **TPR** (Total Physical Response).

One of the most successful approaches to teaching English to language support children is Total Physical Response. At the heart of this approach is the belief that children should be active participants—as both fellow learners and experts—in learning communities where language and content are developed together.

Total Physical Response

TPR:

- is most appropriate for children just beginning to speak English. It recognizes that children will spend a period of time—the silent period—listening to English before they are able to speak it. Particularly focused TPR activities help ESL children learn vocabulary and concepts.

- recognizes that ESL children can understand physical prompts and can indicate their understanding through action before speech. TPR involves giving commands in which you model a physical action and to which learners respond with an action, one or two words, or short responses.

- allows children to involve their bodies and their brains in the TPR activity; they respond with the total body. The commands should be fun and should make the second language understandable.

As you work with children needing additional language support , you may find many other ways to use TPR prompts. As children continue to develop their phonological awareness, they will be asked to identify rhyming words, listen for separate syllables in a word, separate the first sound in a word from the rest of the word, and blend sounds together to make words. Recent research findings have strongly concluded that children with good phonological awareness skills are more likely to learn to read well. These lessons will help you work with children from diverse cultural and linguistic backgrounds as well as engage ESL children in productive activities to achieve literacy.

Develop Visual Literacy (Grades 3-6)

The Language Support Manual expands this lesson by suggesting physical activities which help clarify the Comprehension Strategy Objective stated in the Teacher's Edition. This section also presents an opportunity to involve the ESL student with discussion prompts which explore the individual students cultural background and uses their prior knowledge to do a compare and contrast activity which will assist in introducing the lesson content.

Read the Literature

This section introduces the unit concepts and the vocabulary needed to understand them.

Vocabulary

Suggestions are given here for teaching the vocabulary strategies highlighted in the Teacher's Planning Guide. Notes may call attention to idioms, figurative language, or language special to the selection. The vocabulary words are included, together with questions and tips for helping children increase comprehension.

An example activity from the grade one lesson for *Sam's Song* follows:

Invite children to play a game of "Find the Word." Organize the group into two teams. Write the vocabulary words on the board for both teams. Then invite one child from each team to the board and ask them to erase the word you call out. If a child erases the incorrect word, rewrite it. Play until one team erases all the words.

Evaluate Prior Knowledge

Building background is particularly important when children's cultural diversity interferes with comprehension. It is equally important to bring the reading topic to life—give it some immediate relevance—when it is unfamiliar to those children.

Recognize different prior knowledge bases; use familiar contexts to introduce unfamiliar topics.

This section of the lesson includes activities to help children get to know something about the cultural traditions and beliefs that move the story along and that may influence characters' actions. It is important to remember that ESL children's prior knowledge bases were not developed around the cultural traditions of English. They need help developing strategies to activate their own prior knowledge, so crucial to constructing meaning. Recognize that it takes time to learn concepts using a familiar language, let alone a new one.

Model the language and use props when possible.

The activities in this section help ESL children deal with culturally unfamiliar topics by giving it a familiar context. The concept is brought to life as children are encouraged to draw upon their personal experience and knowledge to get the big picture. Role-playing, objects, story props, pictures, gestures, stories with practicable patterns, and story maps are used in many of the activities to help set the topic in a meaningful context.

The concept of learning something new is addressed in the grade one selection *Sam's Song.* An example from this section follows:

Ask children to name things they have recently learned to do or would like to learn to do. Write their responses on the chalkboard. Ask one child to work with you as you model teaching how to do one of the activities. For instance, you might help a child learn to tie her or his shoe.

Next invite children to work in pairs to learn something new from each other. They can learn something real, such as making a paper airplane, or pretend to learn something, such as how to drive a car.

Develop Oral Language

In the grade one selection, *Sam's Song,* children build background by focusing on the concept learning something new. It is important to help children become active participants in learning and confident language users. The activities in this section offer opportunities for children to respond orally to activities more suited to their abilities.

This part of the lesson also offers suggestions for TPR commands you can use when teaching story concepts. Like their English-speaking classmates, ESL children will be at different levels of language and literacy proficiency in their native language. They will also be in various stages of English language acquisition.

Guided Reading

Preview, Predict, Read In *Sam's Song,* children are guided through a picture walk of the book. As children are directed to look at the illustration, they are asked questions, such as: *What do Chuck, Mom, and Pop do under the moon? Who watches them sing? Why do you think Sam looks sad? What does Sam finally learn to do? How do you think he feels?* Based on the children's abilities, they are called on to give short answers.

Graphic Organizer A graphic organizer which follows each reading selection is designed to engage children in active learning. In the grade one selection, *Sam's Song,* a "Story Puppets" blackline master is available. Children are asked to color the pictures of Sam and his family and then cut them out. The pictures are glued to craft sticks and used as puppets. The children work in groups of four and use the puppets to act out the story as you reread *Sam's Song* aloud.

Engage children in active learning.

Build Skills

Blackline Masters

This section contains directions for using the blackline masters as well as informal assessment suggestions.

Phonics and Decoding (Grades 1-2)

This section of the Language Support lesson provides suggestions and activities to help children acquire phonics and decoding skills. Like other sections of the lesson, it follows the Teacher's Planning Guide materials, modifying them and adapting them where possible or providing alternative approaches to the skill that are more appropriate for second-language learners. It covers:

Comprehension and Vocabulary Strategy

This section offers suggestions to help children develop comprehension and vocabulary skills throughout the selection. Lessons encourage you to ask simple questions that draw upon the children's own experiences, cultures, and ideas. The blackline masters give the students additional practice for each assessed skill introduced in the reading selection.

In the grade one selection, *Sam's Song,* the comprehension skill, Compare and Contract, is reviewed. Children are asked to use the story illustrations to help them find similarities and differences in the story. For example, children are directed to a page in the story, then asked: *Is Sam like the mouse? How is she different from the mouse?* Children then work in pairs to compare similarities and differences that they find.

Informal Assessment

After each skill or strategy has been practiced with the blackline master the Language Support Manual includes an informal assessment activity which requires the students to return to the reading selection and apply the skill.

THE WISE OLD WOMAN pp. 18A–43P

Retold by Yoshiko Uchida Illustrated by Martin Springett

BUILD BACKGROUND FOR LANGUAGE SUPPORT

I. FOCUS ON READING

Focus on Skills

Develop Visual Literacy

OBJECTIVE: Identify problem and solution

TPR

Write the following equation on the board: *3 + 1 = ?*. Ask a volunteer to solve the problem. Repeat with another simple equation. Point to each part of the equation and ask students to raise their hands when you point to the problem and to clap when you point to the solution. Explain to students that many stories focus on a problem which must be solved. Finding the solution may constitute the main events of the story. Then direct students' attention to the page from *Court of Alexander the Great.* Have students name as many things at they can in the picture. If necessary, use prompts to start the activity: *Who do you think is sitting in the big chair? What do we call this kind of chair? Point to a lady in a red dress. Do people dress like this now? When do you think the scene takes place? Then ask: Why might people go before a king? How could a king help people?* Invite students to dramatize the picture. Have one student act as the king, while other students pretend to be the king's subjects. Invite students to brainstorm problems one might bring to a king for him to solve. Have students present their "problems" to the king, and allow the king to offer "solutions." For example, a student could point to their untied shoelaces and the king could tie them. Allow various students to play the king. Then have students return to the painting. Invite them to guess what problem the king might be trying to solve.

II. READ THE LITERATURE

Vocabulary

VOCABULARY
conquered
banner
summoned
scroll
reluctantly
prospered

Print each vocabulary word on a flashcard. Display the flashcard for a word as you read aloud the sentences from Teacher Chart 2. Invite students to identify the context clues in each sentence and guess the meaning of each vocabulary word. Have them role-play and/or use props to demonstrate their understanding of the words:

conquered: Show me how you would feel if enemies <u>conquered</u> your country.

banner: Draw a picture of a <u>banner</u>.

summoned: Show me how the king <u>summoned</u> the messenger.

scroll: Use a piece of paper to make a <u>scroll</u>.

reluctantly: Give me a piece of paper. Now show me how you would <u>reluctantly</u> give me the paper. When you do something <u>reluctantly</u>, do you want to do it?

prospered: Show me how people in the castle might look when they have <u>prospered</u>. Are they happy or sad?

Then have students get together in small groups and give each group a flashcard. Have students work together to come up with a definition for their word. Then have each group present its word and definition to the rest of the class.

Evaluate Prior Knowledge

CONCEPT
wisdom and age

Display a group of photographs showing people at various ages. Try to include pictures such as a baby, a toddler walking, a child riding a bike, a teenager driving a car, a teacher, and other professionals. Ask questions to prompt discussion of the wisdom that comes with age and experience. Point to the appropriate picture to identify the life stage you are discussing. Ask: *Do you think a baby knows as much as you do? This toddler knows how to walk. Does he/she know more than the baby? Does the boy/girl driving a car know more than the boy/girl riding a bike? Do you think you know as much as your parents do? Do you think older people are wise? Why? Do you think you know more now than you did when you were younger?* Then have volunteers tell or pantomime for the class something they know how to do. Ask volunteers to tell the class who taught them how to do what they learned. Then have students gather in small groups to role-play a situation in which someone teaches something to someone else. Have students use the photographs as sign-boards to adopt the roles of people at different ages.

Develop Oral Language

nonverbal prompt for active participation

one- or two-word response prompt

prompt for short answers to higher-level thinking skills

prompt for detailed answers to higher-level thinking skills

- Preproduction: *Point to the picture* (gesture to photos) *which shows how old your character is. Show us what you are learning or being taught.*

- Early production: *Point to the picture of the age of the person who taught you something. Can you name what you learned?*

- Speech emergence: *Does the age of the person who teaches you matter? Why or why not? Do you think a younger person might be able to teach the same thing?*

- Intermediate fluency: *Tell me why the older person knew how to do the thing he/she taught you. Do you think older people are wise? Tell us about an older person you admire. Why do you admire her or him?*

Guided Instruction

Preview and Predict

Read aloud the selection title, and ask students to predict what the story will be about. As you lead the class on a picture walk, ask questions that prompt more predictions and reinforce the concepts of wisdom and age: *Who do you think these people are? Why do you think the man is carrying the old woman? Where do you think they are going? What is the man doing in this picture? Who do you think the men on horses are? How do you think the man in the picture feels? What do you think the woman is doing with the rope?*

GRAPHIC ORGANIZER
Blackline Master 1

Objectives

- To identify problems and solutions
- To understand story events
- To work cooperatively

Materials

One copy of Blackline Master 1 per student; pencils

Ask students to fill out the Blackline Master as they read the story. Explain to students that the characters in the story will encounter problems and attempt to solve them. Tell students that as they read they will keep track of each problem the character faces; his/her attempts to solve the problems; the outcomes of those attempts; and the final solutions. You may want to discuss each problem/solution with the class before they write it in the chart. Or, have students work together to complete their charts.

Reinforce the skill of identifying problems and solutions. Have students prompt each other by citing a problem or solution from each other. Have partners identify the solution that solved the problem or the problem which needed the solution.

III. BUILD SKILLS
Comprehension

REVIEW PROBLEM AND SOLUTION
Blackline Master 2

Objectives
• To identify problem and solution
• To recognize story events

Materials
One copy of Blackline Master 2 per student; pencils

Review story events with students. Then explain to students that each picture on the worksheet represents a solution from the story. Help students read each sentence aloud. Explain to students that each sentence describes a problem from the story. Then have students draw lines connecting each problem to its solution. Then have students discuss the answers.

INFORMAL ASSESSMENT

Read aloud the second paragraph on page 26 of the selection. Ask: *What problem did the farmer solve by having his mother live in the cave?* (By hiding his mother in the cave, the farmer kept his mother safe from the cruel lord's law requiring all older people to be left in the mountains to die.)

Comprehension

INTRODUCE MAKE INFERENCES
Blackline Master 3

Objectives
• To develop the skill of making inferences
• To encourage critical thinking

Materials
One copy of Blackline Master 3 per student; pencils

Explain to students that as they read, they can make inferences, or guesses, about how characters in the story feel. Direct students' attention to the drawings at the bottom of the sheet. Have them read the label under each drawing, explaining that each face portrays a different emotion. Then read the questions aloud. Ask students to draw faces similar to those at the bottom of the page to show how they think the story characters felt. Discuss students' answers. Point out that more than one answer could be correct for each question.

INFORMAL ASSESSMENT

Remind students of the three impossible tasks Lord Higa required in order to spare the cruel young lord and his village. Ask: *How do you think Lord Higa felt when the tasks were completed successfully? Why do you think he felt that way?*

Vocabulary Strategy

**INTRODUCE ANTONYMS
AND SYNONYMS**
Blackline Master 4

Objectives
• To develop understanding of synonyms and antonyms
• To reinforce vocabulary

Materials
One copy of Blackline Master 4 per student; pencils

Read aloud the words in the boxes. Explain that for each word in box 1, there is a word with the opposite meaning in box 2. Model by providing a simple antonym pair, such as hot/cold. As a class exercise, have students identify the antonym pairs. Then have students complete their sheets by writing the words in the spaces provided. Explain that the ≠ sign means "not equal to," or "not the same."

INFORMAL ASSESSMENT

To assess understanding of antonyms, have students turn to p. 22 and read the last sentence on the page. Point out the word *early*. Ask students to think of an antonym for *early* (*late*). Repeat the exercise with the word *softly* on the same page.

Problem and Solution

Problems

⬇

Attempts

⬇

Outcomes

Match the Solution to the Problem

1. Draw lines to match each problem with its solution.

Problem	**Solution**

The young farmer must find his way home.

The young lord must make a coil of rope out of ashes.

The young lord must run a thread through a crooked log.

The young lord must make a drum that sounds without being beaten.

How Did They Feel?

Using the examples below, draw faces to show how each person felt.

1. How did the farmer feel when he took his mother to the mountains?

2. How did the young lord feel when the warriors galloped into his village?

3. How did the old woman feel when the young lord gave her three bags of gold?

happy

sad

frightened

angry

Memory Game

1. Look at the words shown below. **2.** Each word in box #1 has an opposite in box #2.
3. Find the opposite of each word and write them in the space provided.

Box #1

wise	reluctant	win	short	young	done

Box #2

tall	stupid	old	incomplete	lose	eager

1. _____ ≠ _____

2. _____ ≠ _____

3. _____ ≠ _____

4. _____ ≠ _____

5. _____ ≠ _____

6. _____ ≠ _____

THE VOYAGE OF THE *DAWN TREADER* pp. 44A–65P

Written by C. S. Lewis Illustrated by Amy Hill

BUILD BACKGROUND FOR LANGUAGE SUPPORT

I. FOCUS ON READING

Focus on Skills

OBJECTIVE: Analyze character and setting

TPR

Develop Visual Literacy

Point to yourself and say *Who am I?* (teacher). *Where am I?* (in the classroom). Explain that in stories characters are the *who* and the setting is the *when* and *where* the story happens. Explain to students that many paintings and photographs focus on a character or characters in a particular setting. Turn students' attention to the painting *Cliffs of the Upper Colorado, Wyoming Territory*. Have students point to elements in the painting which make up the setting, such as the cliffs, river, clouds. Prompt discussion: *What's happening in this picture?* (Point to a dark cloud.) *Does this picture look like the place where you live? Does the picture look like a storm is coming? What are the people doing? How do you think they feel? How can you tell? Do you think they know a storm is coming? How would you feel if you were a character in this setting? Show me. What colors does the artist use? Why do you think he used those colors?* Invite students to draw a picture with a different setting, but similar characters. Encourage them to discuss the differences between their drawings and the Thomas Moran painting.

II. READ THE LITERATURE

VOCABULARY
vaguely
approve
bruised
convenience
offend
presence

Vocabulary

Print the vocabulary words on the chalkboard, and introduce their meanings by reading the sentences on Teaching Chart 8. Then make the following statements: *Some people vaguely remember things that happened to them as babies. We must all take care not to offend others. A bruised leg takes time to heal. The presence of the police makes people feel safe. To show that they approved of the play the audience gave the cast a standing ovation. Public transportation is a convenience for people who don't have cars.* Help students build understanding by developing their own context clues for each word. Begin by encouraging students to guess what the words mean. Record their suggestions on the chalkboard. Then invite student pairs or groups to suggest—with words or gestures—a context clue for the word. Poll students on whether to accept the clue. Continue until several clues exist for each word. Then have students take turns at the chalkboard, drawing lines from context clues to the correct word. Invite students to use the words to create a one-paragraph description of a recent class activity.

CONCEPT
boats and ships

Evaluate Prior Knowledge

Bring in as many pictures of boats and ships as possible. Tape these pictures on the right side of the chalkboard. Write *boats* and *ships* on the left side of the chalkboard leaving enough room to place the correct pictures under the headings. Discuss how a boat is different from a ship (ships are bigger and carry more people, some boats don't have engines and use sails to move from point to point, and so on) Ask students to decide what each picture on the board is, a boat or a ship. Have volunteers take individual pictures and place them under the correct heading on the board. Tell students about boats and ships familiar to you, using the pictures. For example, hold up a picture of a ferryboat, and explain that ferries take people and cars across rivers and bays. A yacht is a luxury boat that is used for racing, cruising and especially for pleasure. A cruise ship often has many decks, a pool, bars, restaurants, shops, and carries many people to visit different places around the world. As students post pictures into the two categories, help them identify similarities and differences between ships and boats. Ask students what kinds of boats they have seen.

TPR

Develop Oral Language

Invite students to tell about or draw boats and ships they have seen. Encourage them to describe the boats and ships—using the pictures on the board if necessary—adding any personal experience traveling on water. Provide vocabulary as needed.

nonverbal prompt for active participation

• Preproduction: *Show us* (point to self and class) *your picture. Does it show a ship? Does it show a boat?* (Model yes or no with head movements.) *Point to the* (front, back, sails, and so on) *of the boat. Show us how your body moves when you are on a boat.*

one- or two-word response prompt

• Early production: *Is this a* (type of boat or ship)*? What color is it? Is it very big? Have you ever been on a boat or ship like this?*

prompt for short answers to higher-level thinking skills

• Speech emergence: *What kind of boat or ship is that? Where did you see it? Did you ride on it? Do you like riding on boats or ships?*

prompt for detailed answers to higher-level thinking skills

• Intermediate fluency: *Tell us about a boat or ship you saw or rode on. How big was it? What did you enjoy about riding on the boat or ship?*

Guided Instruction

Preview and Predict

Tell students that this story is about a sister and brother who have wonderful adventures in a land called Narnia. Explain that Lucy and Edmund can go to Narnia only by magic. Also tell students that Eustace (the third person in the story) doesn't believe in Narnia but he's in for a surprise. Pair less proficient speakers with fluent ones to preview the story illustrations. As you discuss the illustration with students, ask questions such as: *What kind of boat do you think this is? Have you ever seen a boat like this? What color is the sail? Why do you think the children are looking at the painting on the wall? What do you think is happening to the girl? Do you think it is magic? Why? What do you think has happened to the children now? Do you think they are on their way to Narnia? Why or why not? Do they look scared or happy when they find themselves on the ship? Do they know the person they are greeting? How would you feel if this happened to you? How do you think the girl feels about the mouse?*

GRAPHIC ORGANIZER
Blackline Master 5

Objectives

• To analyze character and setting of a story
• To practice critical thinking
• To make inferences

Materials

One copy of Blackline Master 5 per student; pencils

Explain to students that paying attention to the characters and the setting will help them understand the story. Students can use the text and the accompanying pictures to make notes on the characters and how they change throughout the story. As students read, have them make notes on the main characters, including physical descriptions and the emotional feelings the characters express. Do the same with the setting of the story. Have students volunteer answers as you prompt them with questions, such as: *Who is Eustace? How does he feel about Narnia? Who is Caspian? How do Lucy and Edmund feel about him?* To help students reinforce the skill of identifying character and setting, ask them to role-play a character from the story. Urge them to show setting through gesture or character reaction.

III. BUILD SKILLS

Comprehension

REVIEW STORY ELEMENTS
Blackline Master 6

Objectives
- To identify story elements
- To broaden understanding of character and setting
- To practice following directions

Materials
One copy of Blackline Master 6 per student; pencils

Discuss the story characters with the class and have students brainstorm words that describe the characters. Write the words they suggest on the chalkboard. Have students complete the web on their sheets by writing one or two words that they think best describe each character. Acknowledge that answers will vary. Then review the story's setting with students. Have them review the pictures on the worksheet and mark an X on those that represent places in the story. Discuss students' answers when they finish.

INFORMAL ASSESSMENT

To assess students' understanding of setting, have them draw a picture showing one character in the story in a story setting. To assess their understanding of character, have them name their favorite character in the story and explain their choice.

Comprehension

REVIEW MAKE INFERENCES
Blackline Master 7

Objectives
- To practice making inferences
- To develop critical thinking skills
- To reinforce story events

Materials

One copy of Blackline Master 7 per student; scissors; paste or glue

Go over the page with students. Briefly discuss the four pictures, and then read the sentences together. Explain that each sentence goes with only one picture. Have students work in groups of four each responsible for presenting to the class the consensus the group came to on one of the four pictures. Tell students to cut out the sentences, match each sentence to the correct picture, and paste the sentence in the box. Emphasize that they should look carefully at each picture for clues that will help them draw their conclusions. When students finish, ask them what clues they used to match the pictures to the correct sentences.

INFORMAL ASSESSMENT

Have students look at the illustration on page 58. Discuss what inferences they can make about the situation from the picture. For example: *Children are wet and the deck shows no signs of a recent rain, so the children have probably just come up out of the water.*

Vocabulary Strategy

INTRODUCE CONTEXT CLUES
Blackline Master 8

Objectives

• To practice using context clues to understand vocabulary
• To reinforce word identification

Materials

One copy of Blackline Master 8 per student; pencils

Explain that we can often find the meaning of an unfamiliar word by reading the words or phrases around it and looking at illustrations. Have students work independently or in pairs to complete the sheet as you read aloud the words. Read aloud each sentence, giving students time to write their answers before continuing. When students finish, discuss their answers and the clues that helped them respond.

INFORMAL ASSESSMENT

Direct students' attention to page 58, and read aloud what Reepicheep says to Lucy about Eustace. Ask: *What is discourteous? What clues help you understand this word?* Repeat with the word *rummaging* on page 59.

Story Elements

Setting	Character

Visiting the *Dawn Treader*

1. Write one or more words to describe each character. **2.** What would you see if you visited the *Dawn Treader*? **3.** Draw an X next to those pictures that show what you might see.

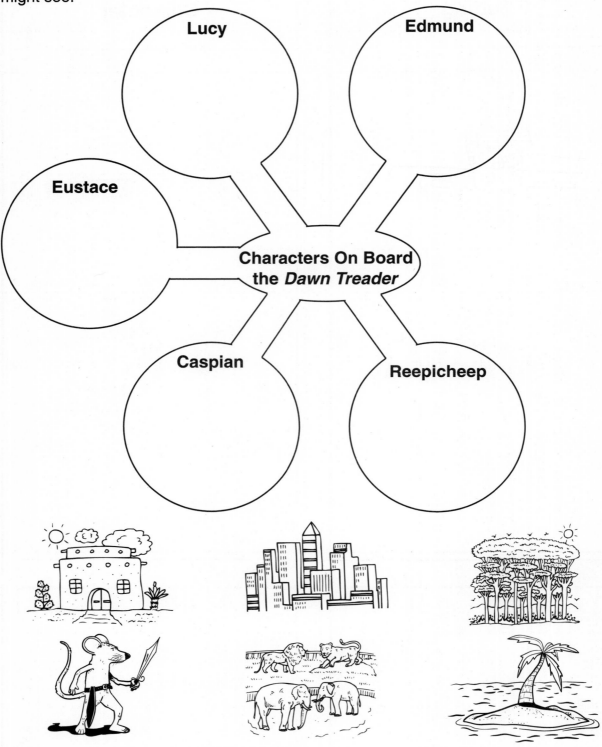

You Know the Answer

1. Cut out the sentences below. 2. Find the sentence that goes with each picture.
3. Paste the sentence in the box.

He is important.

The boats have not returned.

He is not used to being on a boat.

Lunch will be ready soon.

A Day for Adventure

Write the correct word in the blank in each sentence by choosing a word from the list below.

frame	wave	dragon
edge	exciting	annoy-

1. Lucy and Edmund were sitting on the _____ of the

   bed.

2. They were looking at a picture in a gold _____.

3. The picture was of a Narnian ship. The front of it was shaped

   like a _____.

4. Eustace came in and started _____ them, as usual.

5. Suddenly a big _____ took them into the painting.

6. An _____ adventure was about to begin.

WILMA UNLIMITED pp. 66A–93P

Written by Kathleen Krull Illustrated by David Diaz

BUILD BACKGROUND FOR LANGUAGE SUPPORT

I. FOCUS ON READING

Focus on Skills

OBJECTIVE: Identify cause and effect

TPR
Have students use physical response to demonstrate the emotions racing causes in the runners and the audience.

Develop Visual Literacy

Draw two faces on the chalkboard: one showing a person smiling, one showing a person crying. Ask students how they would label these faces. Then say: *What do you think caused this person to smile? What do you think caused this person to cry?* Review with students that a cause is what makes something happen and an effect is what happens. Have volunteers act out or tell a story about what makes them happy or sad. Then direct students' attention to the photograph of Jesse Owens. Tell students that this photograph shows a running race in the Olympics in 1936. Have them point to the runner that they think is Jesse Owens and then to the runner they think will win. Invite students to show elements in the painting that suggest speed and effort. Point out that it looks like the three runners on the left are running just about even in the race. Ask: *How do you think the runners feel? Show us. How do you think the three runners make the leader feel? How do you think watching the race makes the audience feel? Show us.*

II. READ THE LITERATURE

Vocabulary

VOCABULARY
athletic
concentrating
luxury
astounding
bushel
scholarship

Write the vocabulary words on the chalkboard. Lead students in pronouncing each word. Then read aloud sentences from Teaching Chart 14. Ask volunteers to point out context clues. Redirect students to the visual literacy photo on page 66. Ask the following to confirm students' understanding of the vocabulary words: *Do you think the runners are concentrating on winning? How would concentrating, or thinking hard, about winning help in a race? Do you think these runners could get athletic scholarships to go to school? Why would a school with a good athletic program want runners? How would a scholarship help a runner with little money go to school? Do you find it astounding that these four runners are so close to each other? Name something else in the photo that you find astounding. Runners like Jesse Owens can win many medals. Do you think a bushel basket would be a good place to keep all the medals? How many medals do you think would fit in a bushel basket? Do you think Jesse Owens has the luxury of slowing down? If the other runners were farther behind, would he have the luxury of slowing down?* Then have students get together in small groups and have each group choose a different vocabulary word. Have students look through magazines to find pictures illustrating their group's vocabulary word. As a group, have students write a context sentence for the picture using the vocabulary word. Have groups take turns presenting their word to the rest of the class.

Evaluate Prior Knowledge

CONCEPT
Olympic triumph

Show photographs, filmstrips, or other visual material about the Olympic games. Invite students to identify athletes or flags from their native countries. Then encourage class discussion about students' experiences watching the games on television or in person. Invite students to draw or demonstrate their favorite Olympic events and what they know about famous Olympic athletes. Ask students to share their drawings or demonstrations with the class and to explain why they like a particular sport or athlete.

Develop Oral Language

nonverbal prompt for active participation

- Preproduction: *Show us the athlete in your picture or demonstration. (Model by pointing to the athlete in another picture or demonstration.) Raise your hand if you have seen this athlete or sport at the Olympics.*

one- or two-word response prompt

- Early production: *Is this athlete or sport part of the summer or winter Olympic games? Which do you like best, the summer or the winter Olympic games?*

prompt for short answers to higher-level thinking skills

- Speech emergence: *Which sport do you like best? Why do you like this sport? Can you tell us how it is played?*

prompt for detailed answers to higher-level thinking skills

- Intermediate fluency: *What are the Olympic games? What event or athlete are you showing us? Have you seen this event or athlete outside the Olympic games? Is this event or athlete very popular?*

Guided Instruction

Preview and Predict

Explain to students that they will be reading the true story of Wilma Rudolph's life. Read aloud the selection title and subtitle and ask students to predict what they will learn about Wilma. As students look through the pictures accompanying the story, ask questions to encourage predictions and reinforce the concept of Olympic triumph: *What do you think Wilma did to become known as the world's fastest woman? What do you do when you want to win? Who do you think that man is with Wilma and her mother? What do you think is wrong with Wilma? What is Wilma wearing on her legs? What do you think she's thinking about as she watches the other children? How do you feel when you are left out of a group? Do you think Wilma will win the race?*

GRAPHIC ORGANIZER
Blackline Master 9

Objectives

- To identify cause and effect
- To understand story events
- To work cooperatively

Materials

One copy of Blackline Master 9 per student pair; pencils

As students read the story, have them work with a partner to identify cause-and-effect relationships described in the text. Pair students with limited verbal and writing skills with more fluent English speakers. Suggest that one student record the answers. After students finish reading the story, have them share their charts with the class. Reinforce cause and effect through role-play. Have students demonstrate a cause-effect relationship, such as Wilma's illness and subsequent handicap.

III. BUILD SKILLS
Comprehension

REVIEW CAUSE AND EFFECT
Blackline Master 10

Objectives
• To review cause and effect
• To recognize the sequence of events

Materials
One copy of Blackline Master 10 per student; scissors; paste or glue

Discuss with students how one event can cause a series of other events. Explain that we call this a chain reaction, because the events are connected like the links in a chain. Review the worksheet with students and point out how the boxes are displayed to show such a series of events. Read aloud the directions, the events in the chart, and the sentences above the chart. Have students work independently or in pairs to complete the exercise. When students have finished, discuss their answers.

INFORMAL ASSESSMENT

Have students reread p. 73. Then ask students: *What was the effect of Wilma's leg turning inwards?* (She could not move it back) *What was the cause of her sickness?* (polio and scarlet fever).

Comprehension

REVIEW PROBLEM AND SOLUTION
Blackline Master 11

Objectives
• To review problem and solution
• To understand story events

Materials
One copy of Blackline Master 11 per student; scissors; paste or glue

Go over the worksheet with students. Explain that the boxes on the left column will show "What Wilma Does" to solve her problem and the boxes on the left show "What Happens" as a result of what Wilma does. Read aloud the sentences in the chart and the sentences above the chart. Have students write the sentences in the correct spaces in the chart. When they finish, review the answers. Ask students to name other things Wilma did to solve the problems caused by polio.

INFORMAL ASSESSMENT

Have students turn to p. 76 and reread the last paragraph. Ask students: *What did Wilma do to make her knees stop trembling?* (She concentrated on her breathing).

Vocabulary Strategy

REVIEW CONTEXT CLUES
Blackline Master 12

Objectives

• To review context clues
• To associate vocabulary with pictures

Materials

One copy of Blackline Master 12 per student; pencils

Remind students that pictures which accompany text can sometimes provide clues to unfamiliar words. Read the directions and boxed words aloud to the class. Have students complete the answers independently or with a partner. When they finish, ask volunteers to share their answers. Encourage students to use the words in a sentence.

INFORMAL ASSESSMENT

Write the word *championships* on the chalkboard. Ask students to turn to page 82 and find the word championships in the story. Have them read the paragraph in which the word appears and tell what the word means and the clues that helped them.

Cause and Effect

Cause	Effect

Name_____ Date_____

How Wilma Won

Write the sentences below in the boxes in the order they happened in the story.

Wilma exercises so she can walk without a brace.
Wilma gets polio.
Wilma wins three gold medals.

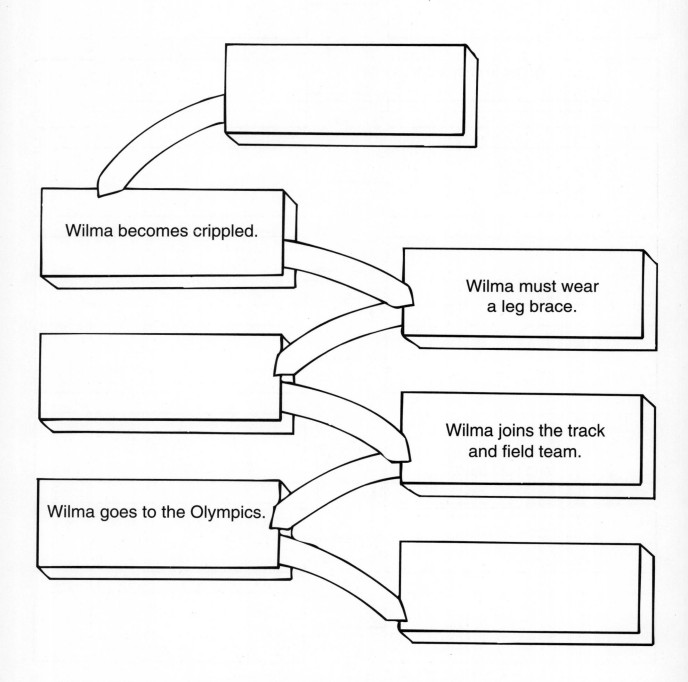

Wilma becomes crippled.

Wilma must wear
a leg brace.

Wilma joins the track
and field team.

Wilma goes to the Olympics.

Wilma Solves a Problem

1. Write the sentences in the correct space on the chart.

Wilma becomes a star athlete.

Wilma's classmates make fun of her.

Wilma does leg exercises.

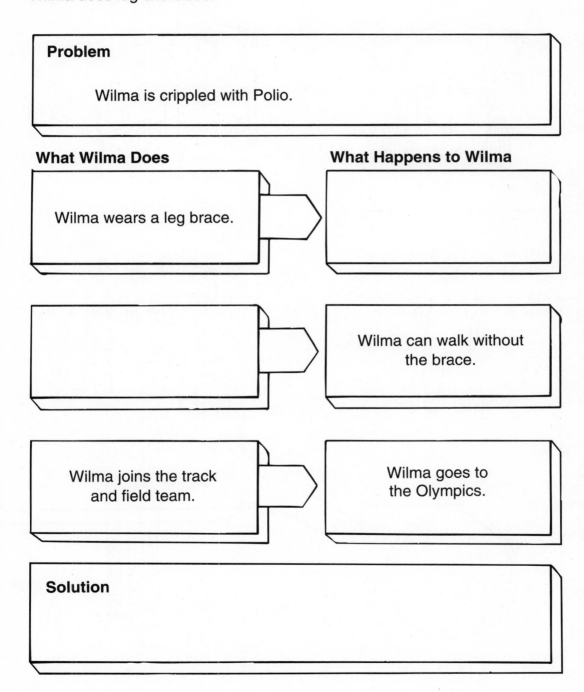

Problem

Wilma is crippled with Polio.

What Wilma Does

Wilma wears a leg brace.

What Happens to Wilma

Wilma can walk without the brace.

Wilma joins the track and field team.

Wilma goes to the Olympics.

Solution

Word Clues

1. Look at the words in the box. **2.** Write the missing letters next to each picture.

pneumonia	luxury	polio	propel	scholarship	exhilarated

s __ __ __ __ __ __ __ s __ __ __

p n __ __ __ __ __ __ __ __

__ __ __ i o

e x __ __ __ __ __ __ __ __ __ __

__ __ x __ __ y

__ __ __ __ __ e l

THE WRECK OF THE ZEPHYR pp. 94A–123P

Written and Illustrated by Chris Van Allsburg

BUILD BACKGROUND FOR LANGUAGE SUPPORT

I. FOCUS ON READING

Focus on Skills

Develop Visual Literacy

OBJECTIVE: Analyze character and setting

TPR

Direct students' attention to the painting on page 94 and then to the painting on page 44. Have them point to similar and contrasting elements. Help students notice that both paintings show people outdoors, but that the settings are very different. Ask, *Is the sea stormy or calm? How can you tell?* Point out, using words and gestures, that the people in the picture on page 94 draw our attention more than those in the other picture. Ask students: *Are the people in the painting happy or sad?* Point out that the title of the picture is *Dad's Coming*, and ask: *Who do you think these people are? What are they doing? Show me how you think they feel. How can you tell? How do you think the characters would feel if the sea was stormy? Why? How would they feel if they saw a ship coming? Show me.*

II. READ THE LITERATURE

Vocabulary

VOCABULARY
spire
shoreline
timbers
treacherous
ominous
hull

Introduce the words by reading the sentences on Teacher Chart 20. Emphasize the vocabulary word in each sentence using physical response, facial expression, and tone as your tools. Read sentences a second time using photographs to help students visualize vocabulary. Invite students to identify context clues that point to a word's meaning. Invite them to suggest definitions and use their definition to replace the vocabulary word in the sentence. Have students check to see if the new definition fits the underlined context clues. To check comprehension, ask the following questions: *Is a spire tall or short? Where do you usually see a spire? Can you find water along a shoreline? Would you find boats or planes along a shoreline? Are timbers made of rock or wood? Is the hull part of a ship or a house? Would you find the sail on a hull? Would climbing a very steep mountain be treacherous? What are some other treacherous activities? Would an ominous sky be blue or gray?*

Evaluate Prior Knowledge

CONCEPT
shipwrecks

Write the word *shipwreck* on the chalkboard. Help students identify and define the two smaller words in *shipwreck* and then define the compound word. Show pictures of famous shipwrecks, such as the Titanic, Andrea Doria, and Lusitania. Ask students to name or draw some possible causes of shipwrecks, such as bad weather, collisions, or being torpedoed. Supply model ships, and have students describe what happened to the ships.

Develop Oral Language

nonverbal prompt for active participation

- Preproduction: *Show us* (point to class and self) *what caused your shipwreck. Model by creating a shipwreck with another boat. Show us what happened to your boat.*

one- or two-word response prompt

- Early production: *What has happened to your boat? What caused this to happen?*

prompt for short answers to higher-level thinking skills

- Speech emergence: *What are some causes of shipwrecks? Which one do you think caused your shipwreck? How might one kind of shipwreck be different than another?*

prompt for detailed answers to higher-level thinking skills

- Intermediate fluency: *What factors add to the chances of a shipwreck? What can the people on a boat do during a shipwreck? What would you do if you were in a shipwreck?*

Guided Instruction

Preview and Predict

Read the selection title and ask students to predict what the *Zephyr* is and what the story will be about. Then explain that in the selection, a boy meets an old man who tells him a story to explain how a sailboat landed on a high cliff. Use the illustration on page 99 to introduce the old man and reinforce the concept of shipwrecks. As you guide students through the illustrations, ask questions that encourage predictions: *What is the old man doing? What is wrong with the sailboat? How do you think the sailboat got where it is? What is the weather like? What vocabulary word describes the sky? Why do you think the boy is lying on the beach? Do you think the story is make believe or real? How can you tell? Where do you think the boy is now? How do you think it ends? Why?*

GRAPHIC ORGANIZER
Blackline Master 13

Objectives

- To analyze character and setting
- To reinforce critical thinking
- To encourage creativity

Materials

One copy of Blackline Master 13 per student; pencils; colored markers or crayons (optional)

After completing the first reading of the story, have students describe the setting and main characters. Write their suggestions on the chalkboard in word webs. Then create a chalkboard copy of the Setting and Character chart, and complete it as a class or with students working in groups of varied fluency.

As a reinforcement, encourage students to draw a picture that shows one story character in the story setting. Invite volunteers to share their drawings with the class.

III. BUILD SKILLS

Comprehension

REVIEW STORY ELEMENTS
Blackline Master 14

Objectives
- To reinforce understanding of setting
- To identify story details
- To provide hands-on experience

Materials

One copy of Blackline Master 14 per student; scissors (optional: paste; tag board; crayons or colored markers)

Have students cut apart the puzzle pieces. Then have them work independently or with partners to complete the puzzle to show a story scene. Point out that there are extra pieces that do not belong in the completed picture. Challenge students to identify these "extra" pieces and explain why they don't fit in the story scene puzzle.

Students can mount their completed puzzles on tag board and color them if they wish.

INFORMAL ASSESSMENT

Ask students to quickly scan the story illustrations. Have them shut their eyes and pretend that they are in the small fishing village of the story. Have them name three things that they might see in the village.

Comprehension

REVIEW MAKE INFERENCES
Blackline Master 15

Objectives
- To practice making inferences
- To promote critical thinking
- To develop skill in analyzing plot

Materials

One copy of Blackline Master 15 per student; pencils

Have students raise their hands to vote "yes" or "no" on whether they think the old man in the story was telling about a dream he had as a boy. Then review the story scenes shown on the page, asking which could happen in real life. Write on the chalkboard *could happen* and *could not happen*. Have students write one of these phrases beneath each picture to identify which scenes could possibly happen in real life. Discuss their answers and whether anything similar to these pictures has ever happened to them.

INFORMAL ASSESSMENT

Read aloud the first sentence on text page 109. Ask: *Why do you think the sailor wanted the boy to leave? Where do you think the sailor lived?*

Vocabulary Strategy

REVIEW SYNONYMS AND ANTONYMS
Blackline Master 16

Objectives
• To recognize antonyms and synonyms
• To build vocabulary
• To build problem-solving skills

Materials

One copy of Blackline Master 16 per pair of students; scissors

Read aloud the words in the circles and squares. Read aloud and clarify the game directions. Have students identify the word pairs with the same meanings. Explain that students will use the cut-out circles and squares to play a game of tic-tac-toe with their partner. If necessary, demonstrate the game by having a student play it with you on the chalkboard.

INFORMAL ASSESSMENT

Direct students' attention to the paragraph at the bottom of page 98, and ask them to read it aloud with you. Have them identify the two words in the paragraph that have the same meaning (story, tale). Then direct students to the first paragraph on page 105, and have them read it aloud with you. Have them identify two words in the paragraph that have opposite meanings (familiar, strange).

Analyze Character and Setting

Setting	Character

Jig Saw Puzzle

1. Cut out the puzzle pieces. **2.** Put the puzzle together. **3.** Hint: Some pieces don't fit.

Was It a Dream?

1. Look at the pictures below. **2.** They are scenes from "The Wreck of the Zephyr".
3. Which scenes show something that did happen in the story. **4.** Write your answers in the space beneath each picture.

Synonym Tic-Tac-Toe

1. Cut out each circle and square. **2.** Play a game with a partner. One player uses the circle words. The other player uses the square words. **3.** Take turns. Put a word on the tic-tac-toe board. **4.** Try to get three words with the same meaning in a row.

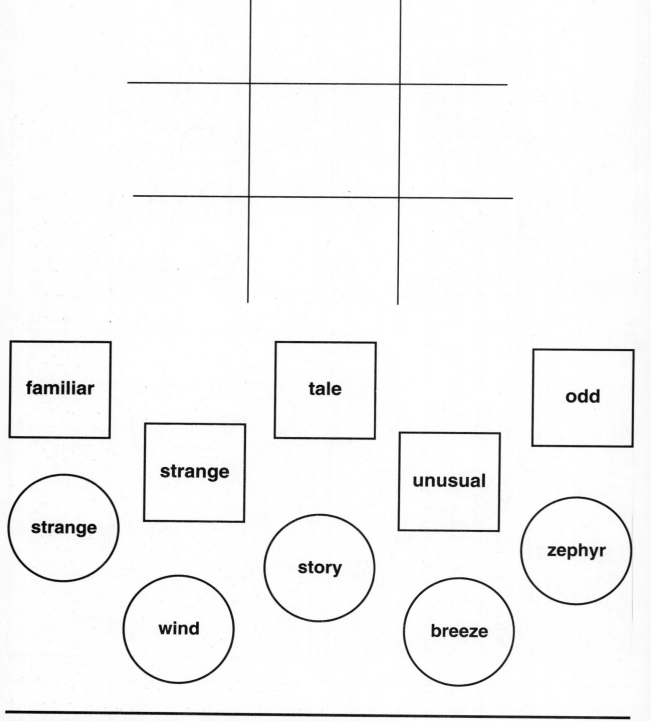

TORNADOES! pp. 124A–133P

Time For Kids

BUILD BACKGROUND FOR LANGUAGE SUPPORT

I. FOCUS ON READING

Focus on Skills

OBJECTIVE: Identify cause and effect

TPR
Have students trace the curved lines of the wave and then demonstrate understanding by showing how the boat's riders feel about the wave.

Develop Visual Literacy

Have students brainstorm words to describe the picture on page 124. Point to the boat, the wave, and the mountain and ask the class to name them. Point out the curved lines of the wave, and help students understand the motion these lines suggest. Then discuss the cause and effect relationships depicted: *What do you think will happen to the boat and the people in it? Show us. What will cause this to happen? Show us in the painting. Why do you think the waves are so high?* Finally, prompt students to describe the effect the picture has on them: *How does this picture make you feel? What parts of the picture cause those feelings?*

II. READ THE LITERATURE

Vocabulary

VOCABULARY
predictions
reliable
detect
severe
destruction
stadium

Read aloud the sentences in Teaching Chart 26. Build additional understanding by reading aloud the selection sentences in which the vocabulary words appear, along with any context clues in the surrounding sentences. Then write each word on a flash card. Have students take turns helping you present a weather forecast. They can hold up the correct word as you say it and then progress to holding up the word when you pause.

The National Weather Service has made new _____ about the weather tomorrow. Their instruments _____ new storms coming in our direction. They now believe these storms may be _____ enough to close roads and airports. These storms may also cause _____ to trees and houses as winds whip across the land. Anyone who needs a safe place during the storm should come to the football _____. Blankets and food will be available there. Stay tuned to this station for _____ updates on this dangerous storm.

To check comprehension, ask the following questions:

detect: If instruments *detect* storms, do they locate them?

predictions: Do *predictions* tell what is going to happen in the future or what happened in the past?

reliable: If predictions are *reliable*, does that mean they are correct or incorrect most of the time?

severe: Is a *severe* storm one we do not have to worry about?

stadium: Is a *stadium* a place where games are played or a place where you go to buy groceries?

destruction: If a storm causes *destruction*, does it cause harm?

Evaluate Prior Knowledge

CONCEPT
severe weather

Display pictures of various kinds of severe weather. Invite students to point out and name weather elements such as wind, rain, snow, or hail. Write their ideas on the chalkboard in the form of a weather word web. Encourage students to describe storms they have experienced. Together, compare the types of storms that occur in different geographic locations. Then organize students into groups to brainstorm elements of a severe storm in your community. Have groups produce a large picture or mural showing the storm and its effect on the community.

Develop Oral Language

nonverbal prompt for active participation

• Preproduction: *Show us* (point to self and class) *the* (rain, snow, etc.) *in your picture. Tell us* (model nodding for "yes" and shaking head for "no") *whether you have ever seen a storm like this.*

one- or two-word response prompt

• Early production: *What kind of weather does your picture show? Can you tell us one problem this weather causes?*

prompt for short answers to higher-level thinking skills

• Speech emergence: *Name as many kinds of severe weather as you can. Which of these does your picture show? What is happening in the picture? How is the community being affected by the storm?*

prompt for detailed answers to higher-level thinking skills

• Intermediate fluency: *Tell us about the worst storm you've ever been in. Was it the storm in the picture? What happened to you during the storm? How do you think people can protect themselves from severe weather?*

Guided Instruction

Preview and Predict

Tell students that this selection is a nonfiction informational article about tornadoes. Have them look at the illustrations and headings on the first page of the selection to predict what the article will tell them about tornadoes. Ask questions that encourage predictions and reinforce the concept of severe weather: *What do you think that funnel-shaped cloud is? What do you think that man is doing in the field? What kind of map do you think this is? Who would use this kind of map? What do you think happened to the church? What do the arrows show in this picture?*

GRAPHIC ORGANIZER
Blackline Master 17

Objectives

• To identify cause and effect relationships
• To understand details

Materials

One copy of Blackline Master 17 per student; pencils

Distribute the blackline master after students have read the article. As a class activity, have students brainstorm the cause and effect relationships in the article. If necessary, prompt them to recognize the following cause and effect events mentioned in the article: tornadoes or severe storms/destruction and death; cold air mixing with warmer air/twister conditions; storm warning/time to get to safety. Write students' suggestions on a chalkboard version of the *Cause and Effect* chart. Have students complete their copies of the chart in pairs, with a more fluent student recording for a less fluent student.

To reinforce the skill of identifying cause and effect, have students draw a two-panel cartoon showing a cause-effect relationship from the article.

III. BUILD SKILLS

Comprehension

REVIEW PROBLEM AND SOLUTION
Blackline Master 18

Objectives
• To reinforce problem solving
• To practice critical thinking
• To understand main idea and story details

Materials
One copy of Blackline Master 18 per student; scissors; paste or glue

Read aloud the sentences before students begin the activity. Tell students to cut out all the boxes and then paste each solution box next to the correct problem. When they finish, discuss the answers and point out that we don't yet know a way to stop tornadoes.

INFORMAL ASSESSMENT
Read aloud the last two sentences of the selection. Ask: *How will advance notice of a storm help save lives?*

Comprehension

REVIEW ANTONYMS AND SYNONYMS
Blackline Master 19

Objectives
• To reinforce story vocabulary
• To explore story details
• To develop word identification

Materials
One copy of Blackline Master 19 per student; pencils

Read aloud and clarify the directions. Then read aloud the first five sentences and the words in the box. Help students choose the word in the box that is a synonym for the underlined word. Repeat the process with the two sentences from the bottom of the page, asking students to find the word from the box that is an antonym for the underlined word. Have students write their answers on the lines provided. Pair students needing language support with more fluent English speakers.

INFORMAL ASSESSMENT
Read aloud the last sentence on page 127. Ask: *What is another word that means the same thing as damage? What is another word that means the opposite of death?*

Vocabulary Strategy

REVIEW CONTEXT CLUES
Blackline Master 20

Objectives

• To reinforce story vocabulary
• To explore story details
• To develop word identification

Materials

One copy of Blackline Master 20 per student; pencils

Tell students to complete the sentences with words from the box. Read aloud the words in the box and each sentence. Then complete the master as a class or have students work with partners, depending on students' language abilities. Invite students to identify the context clues that helped them understand the words.

INFORMAL ASSESSMENT

Read aloud the first two sentences on page 128. Ask students to tell what the word *instruments* means and what clues in the sentences helped them understand the word.

Cause and Effect

Cause	Effect

Storm Warning

1. Cut out the squares. **2.** Match each problem with its solution.

Problem	**Solution**

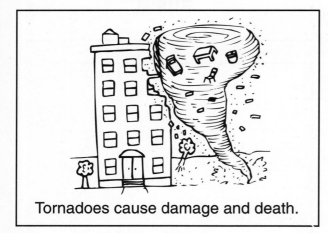

Tornadoes cause damage and death.

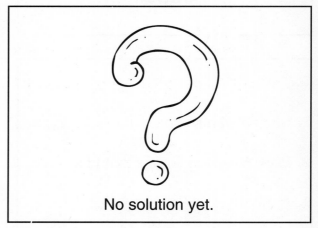

No solution yet.

Problem **Solution**

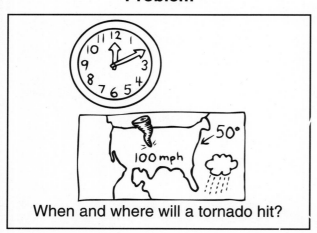

When and where will a tornado hit?

Warn people that a tornado is coming.

Problem **Solution**

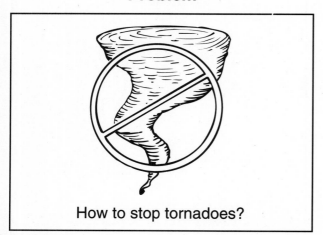

How to stop tornadoes?

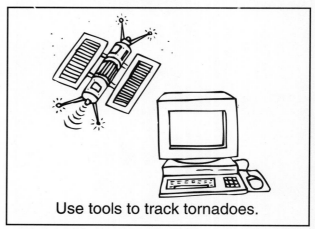

Use tools to track tornadoes.

Same or Opposite?

1. Look at the words in the box. **2.** Then write the word with a **similar** meaning as the underlined word for each sentence.

severe	path	detects	tornadoes	track

1. Twisters are powerful <u>storms</u>. _____

2. No one wants to be in the storm's <u>route</u>. _____

3. Mark Askelson <u>sees</u> a tornado. _____

4. Its damage will be <u>extreme</u>. _____

5. Mark uses a computer to <u>follow</u> the storm. _____

1. Look at the words in the box. **2.** Make each sentence correct by writing the word with the **opposite** meaning of the underlined word.

powerful	danger

1. Tornado alerts warn people that they are in <u>safety</u>. _____

2. Twisters are one of nature's most <u>weak</u> storms. _____

Twister Tracking

1. Look at the words in the box. **2.** Write the correct word in the blanks from the list below.

satellites	radar	destruction	predictions	reliable

1. The tornado tore through the town and caused _____.

2. Scientists use weather _____ as a tool for tracking the storms.

3. _____ is another tool that helps scientists follow a twister's path.

4. Scientists use these tools to make _____ about where and when a tornado will hit.

5. Their predictions are usually very _____.

THE GOLD COIN pp. 138A–165P

Written by Alma Flor Ada Illustrated by Neil Waldman

BUILD BACKGROUND FOR LANGUAGE SUPPORT

I. FOCUS ON READING

Focus on Skills

Develop Visual Literacy

OBJECTIVE: Make predictions

Have students observe the painting on page 138. Conduct a poll by asking students to raise their hands if they see any of the following: a dog, a road, a walking stick, a railroad, a tree, a fire, snow, mountains. Record the items that the majority finds in the painting on the chalkboard. Note the painting's title, and explain that the railroad was not really a railroad, nor did it run underground. Ask them if they can guess how it got that name. Have students then point to and name the elements in the painting from the list on the chalkboard. Then point to the enslaved people and name them. Point to the abolitionists and name them. Explain to students that these were the main elements that made up the underground railroad. Discuss how the railroad helped slaves escape to the North. Ask students to look at the expressions on the faces of the people in the painting and decide if they are scared. Ask students if they think the people are safe. Could they be captured and punished for escaping or helping others escape? Invite students to predict what will happen to the people in the painting.

TPR

Have students use body language to identify elements in the painting and demonstrate the emotions it depicts.

II. READ THE LITERATURE

Vocabulary

VOCABULARY

shriveled
insistent
despair
stifling
speechless
distressed

Read aloud the sentences on Teaching Chart 32 [p. 140D] and the sentences in the text containing the vocabulary words. Then place students in six groups and assign each one a word. Help each group work together to create a dramatization that will characterize the meaning of each word. Give clues to help students develop their skits:

shriveled: (If possible bring a grape and a raisin or pictures of them to class.) A raisin is a shriveled grape. Is a prune a shriveled plum or shriveled orange?

insistent: How do people act when they want something badly? Do they try over and over to get it? Show me what this insistent behavior might look like.

despair: How do you feel when you can't solve a problem? Do you feel anxious and hopeless? Is this despair?

stifling: How do you think you would feel in stifling heat? Would you feel as if you could hardly breathe?

speechless: Speechless comes from the word speak. Can you talk when you are speechless?

distressed: How do you think someone would feel when seeing his or her ruined house? Show me how you think he or she looked. Is he or she *distressed*?

After students finish each skit, have those watching identify the vocabulary word and use it in a sentence to describe the skit.

Evaluate Prior Knowledge

CONCEPT
charity

Help students brainstorm things that people can do to help others. Display or name some charitable organizations that play a role in your community. Invite volunteers to tell about ways they have helped others or been helped by others. Point out that charity involves acts of kindness as well as giving money or other gifts to those in need. It may also involve supporting cultural causes such as dance groups or public concerts. List students' ideas on the chalkboard. Invite them to show, draw, or describe how they think it feels to help someone or be helped by someone. Then have students create a poster showing an act of charity. Posters should show or tell how the people in them feel about the act of charity. Encourage students to use the chalkboard list for ideas. Invite students to share their work.

Develop Oral Language

nonverbal prompt for active participation

• Preproduction: *Point to an act of charity.* (Gesture to posters.)

one- or two-word response prompt

• Early production: *How would you feel if you were* (point to person in poster)? Model showing emotion with body language or facial expression. *Can you tell me one thing about the poster? What does it show?*

prompt for short answers to higher-level thinking skills

• Speech emergence: *How does* (name an organization from the chalkboard list) *help people? How is one person helping another in your poster? What could you do to help others?*

prompt for detailed answers to higher-level thinking skills

• Intermediate fluency: *What would happen without acts of charity? How might people be harmed? What would you do to help charity grow in your community?*

Guided Instruction

Preview and Predict

Distribute copies of Blackline Master 21 so that students can complete it as they preview the story illustrations. Read aloud the title and explain that this story is about a thief who tries to steal a gold coin from an old woman. As you guide students through the illustrations, ask questions to prompt predictions and reinforce the concept of charity: *Where do you think the man is going? What does he find along the way? Why do you think the thief is helping the farmers? How do you think the man feels? What is he thinking? What do you think the farmers will do? Where are these people in the boat going? What do you think Juan is doing with the coin? Why do you think the two men are shaking hands? What do you think the lady is going to do with the gold coin? How do you think the story will end?*

GRAPHIC ORGANIZER
Blackline Master 21

Objectives
• To practice making predictions
• To think creatively

Materials
One copy of Blackline Master 21 per student; pencils

As students preview the story and again as they read, stop at key illustrations so they can predict what will happen next. Have students write their predictions in the left-hand column on the blackline master. If necessary, you may want to pair students of differing language levels and suggest that one student do the recording while the other draws or contributes single words or phrases. After they finish reading the story, have students go back and record what actually happened in the right-hand column of the chart. Discuss their responses. Reinforce the skill of predicting by asking students what they think might happen to the old woman after the story's ending.

III. BUILD SKILLS

Comprehension

REVIEW MAKE PREDICTIONS
Blackline Master 22

Objectives
- To review making predictions
- To practice reading and writing
- To reinforce the story plot

Materials

One copy of Blackline Master 22 per student; pencils; reading textbook

Distribute copies of the blackline master before students begin reading *The Gold Coin*. Point out the page numbers and read aloud the questions beside them. Tell students to stop at the end of each listed page to make their predictions by checking *Yes* or *No*. After students finish reading, have them record what actually happens in the story. Work as a class to compare story predictions with actual story outcomes. Group students as necessary to allow for variations in fluency.

INFORMAL ASSESSMENT

Remind students that at the end of the story Juan gives away the gold coin. Have them predict what happens to Juan next.

Comprehension

INTRODUCE FORM GENERALIZATIONS
Blackline Master 23

Objectives
- To practice form generalizations
- To develop understanding of character
- To reinforce the main idea of the story

Materials

One copy of Blackline Master 23 per student; pencils

Have students circle the pictures that show how Juan looked at the beginning and at the end of the story. Discuss why Juan changed, and then have students write their reason for this change. Help students generalize that a person who does bad only harms herself or himself, but a person who does good for others brings good to herself or himself.

INFORMAL ASSESSMENT

Have students reread page 142. Remind them that Juan goes looking for the woman and along the way meets other people who help him. Ask: *How do you think the story would have changed if the old woman had stayed alone in her hut that night?*

Vocabulary Strategy

INTRODUCE COMPOUND WORDS
Blackline Master 24

Objectives
• To practice forming compound words
• To reinforce vocabulary
• To practice following written directions

Materials
One copy of Blackline Master 24 per student; pencils

Read aloud the words in the boxes. Tell students to match each word in column 1 with a word in column 2 to create a compound word. Model the exercise on the chalkboard with the words *some* and *how*. If necessary, complete the activity orally or assign scribing partners to less fluent students.

INFORMAL ASSESSMENT

Have students scan pages 144, 146, 148, and 150 to find as many compound words as they can. For an added challenge, team students with partners or have them work in small groups to see who can find the most compound words.

Make Predictions

Prediction	What Happens

What Happens Next?

1. Write your predictions.

Page #	What Will Happen	My Prediction		What Happens?
		Yes	No	
160	Will Juan steal the coin?			
162	Will the man and his son help Juan find Dona Josefa?			
170	Will Juan find Dona Josefa at Don Teodosio's House?			
176	Will Juan keep the gold coin?			

Name_____ Date_____

Why Juan Changed

1. How did Juan change? **2.** Draw a circle around the correct picture. **3.** Write your answer in the space provided below.

Juan at the beginning of the story.

Juan at the end of the story.

_____

_____

_____

_____

_____

_____

_____

_____

Compound Word Matchup

1.	some	ball	_____
2.	sun	one	_____
3.	horse	board	_____
4.	cup	bye	_____
5.	country	rise	_____
6.	home	born	_____
7.	foot	back	_____
8.	rain	side	_____
9.	good	coat	_____
10.	new	cooked	_____

JOHN HENRY pp. 166A–199P

Written by Julius Lester Illustrated by Jerry Pinkney

BUILD BACKGROUND FOR LANGUAGE SUPPORT

I. FOCUS ON READING

Focus on Skills

OBJECTIVE: Distinguish between fact and nonfact

TPR
Have students use body language and physical response to demonstrate understanding

Develop Visual Literacy

Ask students if they have ever looked for imaginary things in the shapes made by clouds. Tell them to draw shapes they have seen in clouds that look like something real such as a human face, a dog, or a cat. Then have students look at the painting on page 166. Poll students with a show of hands as to whether they think this picture shows something that could really happen. Have them point to elements in the painting that are real or imaginary, for example, the clouds and the giant. Help them notice that the painting contains both real and imaginary elements. Focus their thinking—through your own gesturing—on the division between the realistic fore-ground and the imaginary background.

II. READ THE LITERATURE

Vocabulary

VOCABULARY
rebuild
acre
dynamite
commotion
pulverized
grit

Place children in groups. Give each group a toy construction set or a few toy con-struction vehicles and blocks for building plus some sand or gravel and a large rock. If possible, show students one of the many computer games about construction, pictures of constructions sites, dynamite, an aerial view of farmland to show acres of land. Ask students to prepare the land for building. First, say, *How will we get rid of this huge rock? Can we use dynamite to explode it?* Then model covering your ears and walking away. Say, *The dynamite makes a loud noise and big mess. Let's cover our ears and get away from the commotion. Now the rock is pulverized. It is smashed into lots of pieces. We can use the grit to cover the driveway.* Model cover-ing your eyes. *Let's be careful not to get the grit in our eyes. It will scratch and hurt. Now that our acre of land is cleared, we can build a farm. There will be lots of room for animals, fields, and buildings on a whole acre of land.* Point to the whole building area to indicate its size. Give students blocks or other building units and ask them to construct a building. Then have them knock it down and build it again. Say, *Your building fell down, please rebuild it. I'd like to see you build it again.*

Evaluate Prior Knowledge

CONCEPT
superhighways

Show pictures (bulldozer, tractor, forklift, a theodolite (measures angles), a computer, construction workers, etc.) or a video of road construction or, if possible, take stu-dents to see some road construction nearby. Ask them to identify the different equip-ment and use gestures to explain how each is used. Then have students draw pictures of the people and equipment required to build a highway. Invite students to display and explain their pictures. If necessary, help them name the equipment and write the words on the chalkboard.

Develop Oral Language

nonverbal prompt for active participation

• Preproduction: *Show us* (point to self and class) *your picture. Is this a picture of a* (dump truck, tractor, bulldozer, construction workers, and so on)*? Have you seen* (insert element from picture) *before? Model nodding for yes and shaking head for no.*

one- or two-word response prompt

• Early production: *What is this machine in your picture? What is it called? Can you tell us one thing about how it is used to build roads?*

prompt for short answers to higher-level thinking skills

• Speech emergence: *What is this* (insert pictured element) *in the picture doing? Where have you seen a* (machine, person) *like this?*

prompt for detailed answers to higher-level thinking skills

• Intermediate fluency: *How is a big road built? Tell us about your picture. What do you like best about the way roads are built? Why?*

Guided Instruction

Preview and Predict

Explain that this story is about a legendary man named John Henry who helped build a road and railway tunnel. As you preview the story with students, ask questions that prompt predictions and reinforce the concept of road and rail construction. Ask: *Where do you think John Henry lived? What are all those animals doing? What do you think John Henry is going to do with that ax? What do you think that man on the horse is going to do? Who do you think those men are in front of the big boulder? Why is John Henry pounding on the boulder? How do you think that road got there? This looks like the White House in Washington, D.C. What do you think it has to do with the story?*

GRAPHIC ORGANIZER
Blackline Master 25

Objectives

• To distinguish between fact and nonfact
• To practice critical thinking
• To recognize exaggeration as a writing style
• To work cooperatively

Materials

One copy of Blackline Master 25 per small group; pencils

After students have read the selection, discuss elements of fantasy and realism to help students understand how some real story elements can be made into imaginary elements through exaggeration. For example, point out that the sun is real, but that it doesn't really wash its face or floss its teeth. As they read, have students work in small groups to complete the chart with lists of story elements that are real or fact and things that are fantasy or nonfact. Tell them to use the question *Could _____ really happen?* as a test. Invite groups to share their lists. Discuss how the imaginary elements of the story make it more enjoyable.

III. BUILD SKILLS

Comprehension

REVIEW DISTINGUISH BETWEEN FACT AND NONFACT
Blackline Master 26

Objectives
• To practice distinguishing between fact and nonfact
• To promote critical thinking
• To reinforce story details

Materials
One copy of Blackline Master 26 per student; pencils

Read aloud and confirm understanding of the directions. Invite students to explain the story episode illustrated in each picture. Have them check real or not real to show whether the episode is something that could or could not happen in real life. Invite students to share and discuss their answers. Talk together about other fact and nonfact elements in the story.

INFORMAL ASSESSMENT

Read aloud the third paragraph on page 188. Ask: *Do you think a machine like that really exists? Do you think one man could really tunnel through a mountain faster than the machine?*

Comprehension

REVIEW FORM GENERALIZATIONS
Blackline Master 27

Objectives
• To review form generalizations
• To distinguish between fantasy and reality
• To practice expressing opinions

Materials
One copy of Blackline Master 27 per student; pencils

Review the directions with students, emphasizing that the goal is to circle the picture students think is the most fun or enjoyable. Stress that students are giving their opinions and that there are no wrong answers for this exercise. Discuss students' completed sheets and encourage them to tell why they like one picture more than another. Help students generalize that exaggeration often makes a story more fun. Some students may generalize that tall tales are silly and they prefer reading about real life events.

Refer students to the superhuman feats on pages 172, 177, 186, and 193. Ask: *Why do you think some people say that John Henry was bigger than life?*

Vocabulary Strategy

REVIEW SUFFIXES
Blackline Master 28

Objectives
• To introduce comparatives and superlatives
• To practice following written directions

Materials
One copy of Blackline Master 28 per student; pencils

Write the words *big, bigger,* and *biggest* on the chalkboard. As you underline the inflectional endings, use classroom objects to demonstrate the comparative and superlative meanings of the words. Have students find other classroom examples to illustrate comparative and superlative words. Then read aloud the words in the left column and point out the three pictures opposite. Tell students to write the correct word under each picture. Depending on students' language ability levels, they may complete the exercise independently or with a partner.

INFORMAL ASSESSMENT
Show students the picture on page 179. Direct them to point to the tallest man in the picture, a man who is taller than the man on the right, the shortest man, and so on.

Fact and Nonfact

Fact	Nonfact

Bigger Than Life

1. Look at the pictures. 2. Check "Real" if the picture shows something that could happen in real life. 3. Check "Not Real" if the picture shows something that could not happen in real life.

Real	Not Real

Tall Tales

1. Draw a circle around the pictures that you think are tall tales. **2.** Talk about what makes the pictures fun.

Big, Bigger, Biggest

1. Look at the pictures. **2.** Write the correct word under each picture.

big,
bigger,
biggest

_____ _____ _____

fast,
faster,
fastest

_____ _____ _____

heavy,
heavier,
heaviest

_____ _____ _____

straight,
straighter,
straightest

_____ _____ _____

strong,
stronger,
strongest

_____ _____ _____

BUILD BACKGROUND FOR LANGUAGE SUPPORT

I. FOCUS ON READING

Focus on Skills

Develop Visual Literacy

OBJECTIVE: Identify main idea

Have students look at the picture on page 200. Ask them: *What do you see in the picture?* As students record responses, list words on the chalkboard. Invite students needing additional language support to point to elements in the painting as you name them. Say: *Point to the ship. Show me the two workers.* Then ask questions to help students identify the painting's main idea: *Are the men in the picture working hard or is the work they are doing easy? How can you tell? What do you think these men are building? Show me in the painting. If you wanted to tell someone what the picture is about, what would you say? Think of one or two words that could tell the whole story of the painting. Now show me small things in the painting that are part of that whole story.*

TPR

Have students use body language physical response to demonstrate understanding.

II. READ THE LITERATURE

Vocabulary

VOCABULARY
auction
dangled
donate
deliveries
lecture
publicity

Introduce the vocabulary words by reading aloud the sentences in Teaching Chart 42 [p. 202D]. As you read the sentences use body language, facial expressions and photographs to help students surmise the meaning. For examples:

auction: Choose an item in the classroom that is very desirable to students and conduct an auction of the item. The price might start at one sentence and go up to a page.

dangled: Show a set of keys dangling from a hook.

donate: Show pictures of a well known charitable organization such as the Salvation Army or UNICEF.

deliveries: Tape a piece of paper to a book and write *Pizza* on it. Leave the classroom with the book. Then knock on the door. When students answer, open the door with the book in one hand and say: *Pizza delivery!*

lecture: Stand at the lectern as if preparing to give a lecture.

publicity: Use something from current events to give an example of someone getting a lot of publicity.

Then read aloud the pertinent sentences from the selection. In both cases, help students identify and understand context clues. Then organize students into small groups and propose the following project:

We're going to plan a "Beautiful Neighborhood" project. We can all donate time to plant flowers or sweep streets. We'll auction off the work on each street. That way people can help improve a street they like. People might pay more if we prepare publicity pictures of our streets. The money can buy us plants and tools.

Encourage students to use the vocabulary words as they contribute their own ideas. Challenge them to think about where plant stores could make deliveries of materials and how they might present their ideas in a lecture to a community audience. Discuss the group's ideas as a class.

Evaluate Prior Knowledge

CONCEPT
kids making a difference

Help students brainstorm ways that they and other children can make a difference in their homes, school, and community. Invite students to the chalkboard to draw pictures of some of the ideas. These might include: caring for neighbors' children, pets, or gardens; helping others with schoolwork; getting food for an older neighbor; collecting items for recycling; and so on. Use props to familiarize students with some of these ideas or others of your own. Prompt further brainstorming with questions: *What kinds of things do you do at home to help your family? Do you do chores or help your sister or brother with homework? Have you ever helped clean up the classroom or schoolyard? Do you recycle paper, cans, and bottles? What other ways do kids help and make a difference in the lives of others?* Invite students to create a poster showing how they can make a difference. Write on the chalkboard the sentence "I can help by _____."

Develop Oral Language

nonverbal prompt for active participation

• Preproduction: *Show the poster of what you can do to help.* (Point to picture.)

one- or two-word response prompt

• Early production: *Have you ever done what this poster shows? How did it make you feel?* (Model showing feelings with facial expressions.) *Who do you think you helped? Show us in the poster.*

prompt for short answers to higher-level thinking skills

• Speech emergence: *How can you make a difference at home? at school? in the community? Which way of helping would you most like to try?*

prompt for detailed answers to higher-level thinking skills

• Intermediate fluency: *What could we do as a class to make a difference at our school? What problems would our work help to solve? How do you think we could get started?*

Guided Instruction

Preview and Predict

Read aloud the title and subtitle of the article and invite students' predictions. Then explain that this selection is a nonfiction article about different ways real children have made a difference in other people's lives. Lead students through the article's pictures, asking questions to prompt additional predictions and reinforce the concept of kids making a difference: *What do you think these tools have to do with the selection? Why do you think there are so many pictures of bicycle tires? What do you think this boy did to make a difference in others' lives? Why do you think this part of the story begins with a picture of a plate of food and some eating tools? What do you think this girl did to make a difference?*

GRAPHIC ORGANIZER
Blackline Master 29

Objectives

• To identify the main idea of a selection
• To recognize details
• To practice form generalizations

Materials

One copy of Blackline Master 29 per student pair; pencils

As students read the article, have them work with a partner to identify the main idea and supporting details. Pair students needing language support with more fluent English speakers. Invite all students to first draw or label with simple words the important ideas in each character's story. Show students how to organize these into one main idea. Then model listing one supporting detail for each character in its own box. Invite partners to share their charts with the class.

To reinforce the skill of main idea and details, invite students to retell the selection to a partner or the whole class.

III. BUILD SKILLS
Comprehension

REVIEW MAIN IDEA
Blackline Master 30

Objectives
- To reinforce the skill of main idea and details
- To practice thinking critically
- To extend the selection

Materials
One copy of Blackline Master 30 per student; crayons or colored markers

Discuss with the class the main idea of the two stories in this article. Help students summarize what Justin Lebo and Dwaina Brooks do to help others. Encourage students to draw pictures showing how Justin helps and how Dwaina helps. Then challenge students to show what they themselves do or could do to help others. Invite students to share their drawings with the class.

INFORMAL ASSESSMENT

Have a student volunteer read aloud the introductory text on pages 204 and 210. Then ask students to tell the article's main idea in one sentence.

Comprehension

REVIEW DISTINGUISH BETWEEN FACT AND NONFACT
Blackline Master 31

Objectives
- To distinguish between fantastic and realistic events
- To encourage critical thinking

Materials
One copy of Blackline Master 31 per student; pencils

Read the title of the blackline master aloud, and then read and review the student directions. Discuss what each picture shows. Direct students to write real or make believe under each picture to tell whether it shows something that could exist in real life or something that could not. Have student volunteers share their answers. Discuss any differences in responses, inviting students to explain their thinking or show elements in the picture that support their choice.

INFORMAL ASSESSMENT

Have students read the selection subtitle and the last three paragraphs of the two stories. Ask: *Are these stories about real things that real people did, or are they make believe?*

Vocabulary Strategy

REVIEW SUFFIXES
Blackline Master 32

Objectives
• To review inflectional endings
• To understand comparisons
• To increase vocabulary

Materials
One copy of Blackline Master 32 per student; scissors

Review, and if necessary clarify, the directions with students. Have students look at each picture as you read aloud the sentence under it. Discuss what the pictures show. Then have students cut out the pictures, mix them up, and then lay them out face up. Challenge students working independently or in pairs to arrange each series of three pictures in correct comparative order. Extend the activity by asking students to hold up pictures in response to your directions: *Show me a good car. Which is the best car?*

INFORMAL ASSESSMENT

Have students flip through the pictures about Dwaina's efforts (pages 210–216). Ask them to draw three pictures: one that they think shows a good meal Dwaina might prepare, one that shows a better meal, and one that shows the best meal.

Main Idea

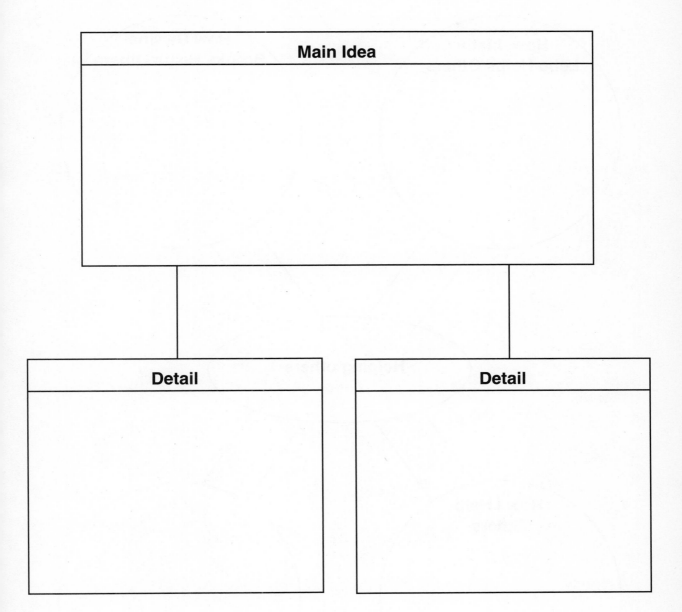

Helping Hands

1. Draw pictures to show how Justin and Dwaina help others. **2.** Draw a picture in the space below to show how you could help others.

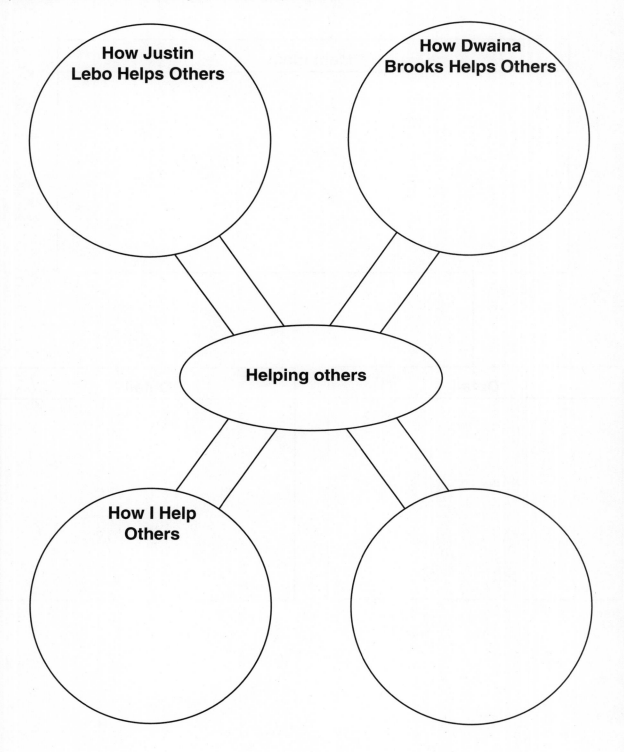

How Justin
Lebo Helps Others

How Dwaina
Brooks Helps Others

Helping others

How I Help
Others

Real or Make Believe?

1. Look at the pictures. **2.** Write the words "real" or "make believe" below each picture.

_____

_____

_____

_____

_____

_____

Good, Better, Best

1. Cut out the pictures. 2. Turn them over and mix them up. 3. Turn each picture over one by one and put them in the correct order.

She is cold.	He is colder.	He is coldest.

He has a good car.	He has a better car.	She has the best car.

It was a bad storm.	It was a worse storm.	It was the worst storm.

DEAR MR. HENSHAW pp. 222A–241P

Written by Beverly Cleary Illustrated by R. J. Shay

BUILD BACKGROUND FOR LANGUAGE SUPPORT

I. FOCUS ON READING

Focus on Skills

OBJECTIVE: Make predictions

TPR
Have students use body language and physical response to identify objects in the picture and show their predictions.

Develop Visual Literacy

Have students bring to class pictures cut out from magazines of people they admire or of things they like. Explain to students that they are going to make a collage of these cut-outs. Point out that the picture on page 222 is made up of many small snapshot-sized photographs pasted together. Help students identify different objects in the picture. Tell students: *Show me a stop sign. Point to another sign.* Read the title *Pear Blossom Hwy.* and challenge students to find a blossoming tree. Ask: *What kind of trees are these? Do you see any pear trees?* Explain that the artist is making a point with the title—perhaps that there were once pear trees but now there is desert. Ask students to make predictions: *Where do you think this road goes? What do you think will happen to this road over time?*

II. READ THE LITERATURE

VOCABULARY
submitted
rejected
reserved
permission
snoop
afford

Vocabulary

Familiarize students with the vocabulary words by reading aloud the pertinent story sentences and the sentences on Teaching Chart 50 [p. 224D]. Emphasize vocabulary and context clues using body language and facial expressions. Then divide the class into six groups and give each a word on a flashcard. Help groups develop a charade or other skit to dramatize the meaning. Challenge other groups to guess the word, using clues provided by the acting group or by you if necessary. Consider these skit ideas along with your own.

snoop: show a spy (or a parent) snooping in search of clues

afford: show a person counting out money and not finding enough at first

submitted: show a girl submitting her poem for the writing contest

permission: show a parent or teacher giving permission to a child to go somewhere

reserved: show a seat with a sign on it and people not sitting in it until the correct person comes to sit in it

rejected: show a committee rejecting an individual's offering

After students seem comfortable with the words' meanings, invite them to write or say captions for some of the skits. Captions should contain one or more of the vocabulary words.

Evaluate Prior Knowledge

CONCEPT
people who inspire us

Help students brainstorm to create a list of people they admire or look up to. Invite them to contribute ideas orally, through pantomime, or using the collage created earlier. Categorize their suggestions on the board in a word web under appropriate headings such as *Athletes, Movie Stars, Politicians, Family Members, Friends, Teachers.* Use pictures where possible to label each heading. Then ask students to draw or bring in a picture of someone who inspires them. In a folded album-style paper, have students paste their picture on one side. Ask them to draw a picture on the other side showing how this person makes them feel.

Develop Oral Language

nonverbal prompt for active participation

- Preproduction: *Show us* (point to self and class) *your pictures. Act out what your hero does to inspire you. Show us* (model using facial expression to show emotion) *how your hero makes you feel.*

one- or two-word response prompt

- Early production: *Tell me one or two things about this person you admire. How does he or she make you feel?*

prompt for short answers to higher-level thinking skills

- Speech emergence: *Who does your picture show? How do you feel about this person? Why do you feel this way? Who are some other people that you admire?*

prompt for detailed answers to higher-level thinking skills

- Intermediate fluency: *What makes this person special? How has this person changed you? What would you like to say to this person?*

Guided Instruction

Preview and Predict

Read aloud the selection title and explain that the story is about a boy who admires a famous author. Distribute copies of Blackline Master 33 so that students can record their predictions as they preview the story. Ask questions that prompt further predictions and reinforce the concept of people who inspire us: *What do you think the boy is thinking about? What might he be writing? Whose picture is this? How do you think the boy feels? Why do you think the story is divided into sections headed by dates? Who do you think these two women are? Why do you think the boy has a scrapbook? Who do you think the people are in these photos?*

GRAPHIC ORGANIZER
Blackline Master 33

Objectives

- To practice making predictions
- To reinforce understanding of story events
- To work cooperatively

Materials

One copy of Blackline Master 33 per student; pencils

Distribute copies of the blackline master before students begin their preview of the story. Have students complete the predictions portion of the graphic organizer chart as part of a story preview exercise. Encourage pantomime or drawings from less fluent students. Record students' responses in a prediction chart on the chalkboard, pausing to discuss any disagreements about predictions. When students have completed their preview, direct them to enter those predictions they agree with on their own sheets. Finally, after reading, tell students to record what really happened in the story on the chart's right-hand column. Again, accept drawings or pantomime from less fluent students. Discuss students' answers as a class, exploring any surprises.

Reinforce the skill of predicting. Have students vote on a likely topic for Leigh's next diary entry.

III. BUILD SKILLS

Comprehension

REVIEW MAKE PREDICTIONS
Blackline Master 34

Objectives
- To practice making predictions
- To reinforce creative thinking

Materials

One copy of Blackline Master 34 per student; pencils

Distribute copies of the blackline master before students begin reading the story. Read aloud the diary date and questions. Direct students to stop after they have read the diary entry listed. Tell them to consider the question and write what they think will happen before continuing reading. Organize students in small groups or pairs to best suit fluency levels. After reading, students can record what actually happened in the space below their predictions. Have a class discussion in which students compare their predictions with what actually happened.

INFORMAL ASSESSMENT

Ask students: *What do you think Leigh will do when he grows up? Why do you think so? What else might Leigh like to be when he grows up?*

Comprehension

REVIEW FORM GENERALIZATIONS
Blackline Master 35

Objectives
- To analyze story characters and form generalizations
- To encourage critical thinking
- To encourage self-expression

Materials

One copy of Blackline Master 35 per student; pencils

Read aloud the directions, pointing out that students' responses may vary. Encourage students to discuss the story events portrayed in the pictures and Leigh's feelings about those events. Have them mark the picture that shows what Leigh feels most strongly about. Ask volunteers to share and explain their choices. If necessary, elicit that Leigh's strongest feelings are about his parents' divorce and missing his dad. Help students generalize that divorce is often hard on children.

INFORMAL ASSESSMENT

Ask students to describe Leigh's feelings toward his mother. Then encourage students to generalize about all children's feelings toward parents.

Vocabulary Strategy

REVIEW COMPOUND WORDS
Blackline Master 36

Objectives
• To practice identifying compound words
• To reinforce vocabulary concepts
• To practice following written directions

Materials
One copy of Blackline Master 36 per student; pencils

Read aloud the directions and the words at the top of the page. Work together to complete the first problem. Then have students complete the exercise independently or with a partner. Review the answers as a class. Invite volunteers to point out the two words that make up each compound word.

INFORMAL ASSESSMENT

Direct students' attention to next to the last paragraph on page 225. Have them identify the compound word (wastebasket, lunchbox) and name the two words it contains. Challenge them to draw a rebus problem for the word. Point out that drumstick has two meanings: the stick for beating on a drum and the leg of a chicken.

Name_____ Date_____

Make Predictions

Predictions	What Happens

What Will Happen?

Diary Entry: Tuesday, March 20
Will Leigh win the Young Writers contest?

My Prediction:

_____
_____
_____
_____
_____
_____

What Actually Happened:

_____
_____
_____
_____
_____
_____

Diary Entry: Sunday, March 25
Will Leigh get to have lunch with a Famous Author?

My Prediction:

_____
_____
_____
_____
_____
_____

What Actually Happened:

_____
_____
_____
_____
_____
_____

Feelings

1. The famous author said that Leigh had strong feelings. **2.** Put a circle around what you think Leigh felt most strongly about.

Word Sums

1. Look at the words in the box below. **2.** Write the word that solves the problem.

| bathroom | yearbook | wastebasket | lunchbox | typewriter |

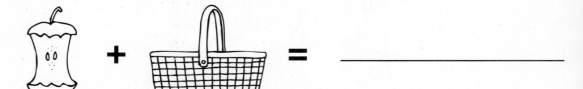

= _____

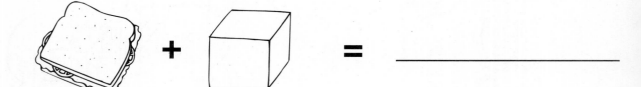

= _____

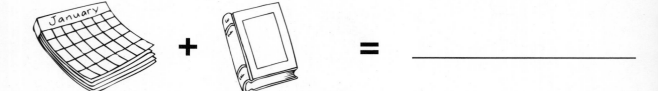

= _____

= _____

= _____

DIGGING UP THE PAST pp. 242A–251P

BUILD BACKGROUND FOR LANGUAGE SUPPORT

I. FOCUS ON READING

Focus on Skills

OBJECTIVE: Identify main idea

TPR

Have students use body language and physical response to demonstrate understanding: *Pretend you are clay soldiers, line up like the soldiers in the photo.* Show us how you can protect the emperor.

Develop Visual Literacy

Organize students into groups using a common characteristic such as clothing design (stripes versus solids). Challenge students to find the common characteristic in each group. Then direct their attention to the photograph on page 242. Explain that it shows a group of clay soldiers found in the tomb of China's first emperor. Invite them to point out features that identify these figures as soldiers. *Why do you think these figures are all dressed alike? Do they look like soldiers in uniforms? What do you notice about the way they are standing? Do they look like marching soldiers?*

Next, explore the main idea of the photo—that the soldiers are there to guard valuables in the tomb and to show what an important person the emperor was: *Do you think an emperor is wealthy and powerful? What else might he have in his tomb? How can soldiers help the emperor protect his tomb?*

II. READ THE LITERATURE

Vocabulary

VOCABULARY
violent
bullet
starvation
arrowheads
fraction
eventually

Write the vocabulary words on index cards and provide students with blank cards or slips of paper. Hold up each card as you say it aloud and read the following sentences to help students with the meaning:

bullet: A gun fires a <u>bullet</u>.

arrowhead: What two words are in this compound word? What is an arrow? Where do you find a head? What do they tell us about the meaning of the compound word?

starvation: Too little food can lead to <u>starvation</u>.

eventually: Something that happens <u>eventually</u> happens after a long time.

fraction: We only know a <u>fraction</u>, or small part, of the story about Jamestown.

violent: Using pistols and knives is <u>violent</u>.

Then read a corresponding pertinent story sentence. Ask students to create flash cards for the word, writing the word on one side and drawing a picture clue on the other side.

Have pairs or groups quiz each other with their picture clues. See who can identify the correct words most quickly. Challenge teams to use each word in a sentence.

Evaluate Prior Knowledge

If possible, display some items from the school's history—awards, photos, yearbooks, and so on. Add your own memorabilia. Then help students draw conclusions about the past from the objects: *Our school was once much smaller. We had a very good basketball team.*

Encourage students to share their experiences viewing objects from the past either in museums or everyday life: *Have you ever discovered old objects buried in the ground? Have you ever found old objects in an attic or old box in your home? How did you find them? What did you find? What did they tell you about the past?*

Fill a box with sand to create a mock dig. Include easily and less easily recognized objects from near and far past—for example, baseball cards, school photos, old tools, pieces of pottery. As students "uncover" items, discuss what each suggests about the people who "left it behind."

Develop Oral Language

Have students bring in photographs and if possible possessions of their grandparents or ancestors.

learning from the past nonverbal prompt for active participation

- Preproduction: *Show us* (point to self and class) *what you found. It looks like a* (name object). *Point to anything similar in our classroom* (indicate classroom and objects).

one- or two-word response prompt

- Early production: *What did you find? Can you name it? Can you tell us or show us how it is used? What else do we have or use today that is like this* (name of object)? *Do we use objects like that today? What kind of clothes are the people in the photographs wearing? Do we wear clothes like that today?*

prompt for short answers to higher-level thinking skills

- Speech emergence: *How is this object the same as something we use today? How is it different? How does the photo show that the way of life was different? How does it show that some things were the same.*

prompt for detailed answers to higher-level thinking skills

- Intermediate fluency: *What can we learn from objects and photographs from the past? What do they tell us about the lives of people who lived before us?*

Guided Instruction

Preview and Predict

Read aloud the title and subtitle of the article and ask students to predict what they will learn. Use the pictures to establish that this selection is a nonfiction article about exploring the past through objects left behind. Then ask questions to prompt predictions and to reinforce the concept of learning from the past: *Where do you think this skeleton comes from? What do you think it can tell us about the past? Where do you think these buildings were? What do you think these round objects are? What could they tell us about the past?*

GRAPHIC ORGANIZER
Blackline Master 37

Objectives

- To identify the main idea and supporting details of a selection
- To reinforce key selection concepts
- To encourage critical thinking

Materials

One copy of Blackline Master 37 per student; pencils

Pair students of varying language abilities so that more fluent English speakers can record answers for the pair. Have students reread the article and discuss what it is mostly about. Write their suggestions on the board. Ask students to give details that support this main idea. When everyone has reached an agreement, write the main idea on the board and ask students to record it on their sheets.

To reinforce the skill of main idea and details, have student pairs create a new cover for the article. Covers should include a title, subtitle, and artwork.

III. BUILD SKILLS
Comprehension

REVIEW FORM GENERALIZATIONS
Blackline Master 38

Objectives
• To encourage critical thinking
• To reinforce lesson concepts
• To practice working cooperatively

Materials
One copy of Blackline Master 38 per student; pencils

Ask students to look at the comic strip panels and discuss what each panel shows. Explain that the children shown are looking at things stored in an attic trunk. Then point out the four people pictured at the bottom of the sheet. Ask students to draw lines matching the objects in the trunk with the people who most likely used the objects. In discussion, help students generalize that we can learn things about people by examining things they own or use. Have students suggest what these objects may tell about each person.

INFORMAL ASSESSMENT

Read aloud the third paragraph on page 247. Ask: *Why do these objects tell the story of a violent time? How were these objects used?*

Vocabulary Strategy

REVIEW COMPOUND WORDS
Blackline Master 39

Objectives
• To practice identifying compound words
• To reinforce vocabulary concepts
• To expand vocabulary knowledge

Materials
One copy of Blackline Master 39 per student; pencils

Read aloud the words at the top of the page. Remind students that a compound word is a word made up of two smaller words. Have students circle each compound word. Ask volunteers to share their answers and identify the two words that make up each compound word.

INFORMAL ASSESSMENT

Have students find the compound words on page 245. Encourage students to name and define the two words that make up each compound word.

Vocabulary Strategy

REVIEW INFLECTIONAL ENDINGS
Blackline Master 40

Objectives
- To review inflectional endings
- To practice following written directions
- To reinforce vocabulary concepts

Materials

One copy of Blackline Master 40 per student; pencils

Read aloud the directions and explain that they apply to all three sections. Then read aloud the words and sentences in each of the three sections. After you read each sentence, allow time for students to write their answers. Invite volunteers to share their answers.

INFORMAL ASSESSMENT

Read aloud the sentences on pages 245 and 247 containing the words *first*, *washed*, and *knowing*. Omit these words when you read. Ask students to choose the correct word from these pairs first last; *washed wash*; and *know knowing* to finish each sentence.

Main Idea

Details

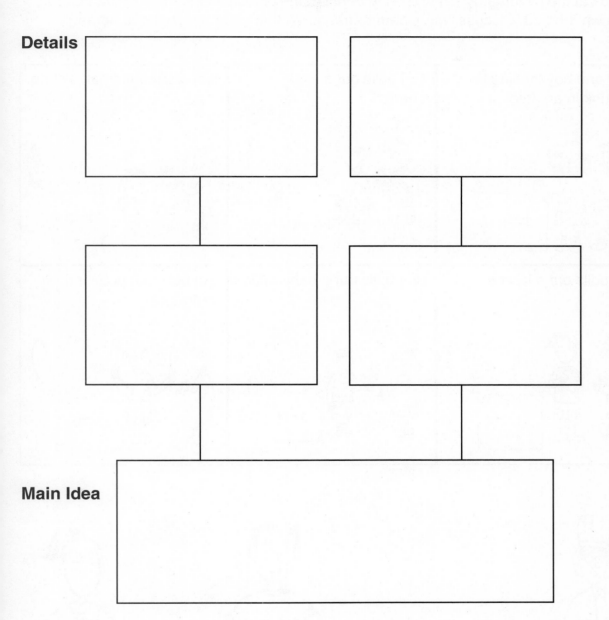

Main Idea

Treasure Talk

1. Look at the pictures. **2.** Draw lines to connect the objects in the trunk to the people who own them. **3.** Discuss with a partner treasures that you have found at home.

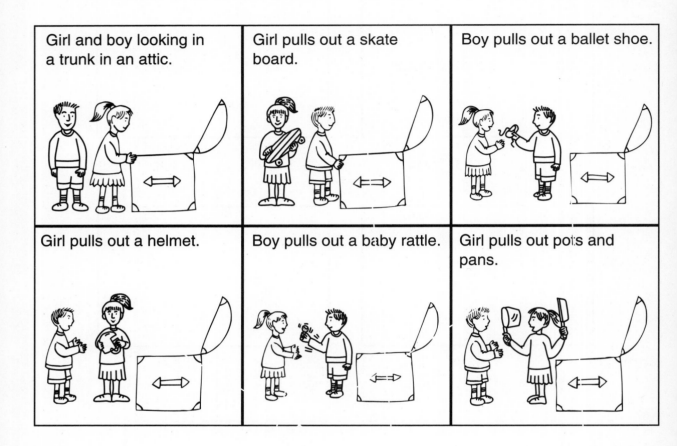

| Girl and boy looking in a trunk in an attic. | Girl pulls out a skate board. | Boy pulls out a ballet shoe. |
| Girl pulls out a helmet. | Boy pulls out a baby rattle. | Girl pulls out pots and pans. |

Word Search

1. Draw a circle around each compound word.

candlesticks	arrowheads	starvation	settlers
bullet	skeleton	Jamestown	underground
triangle-shaped	fraction	violent	helpful
shoreline	attic	wilderness	coin
website	eyeglasses	basketball	discover

Word Endings

1. Look at the words in the boxes. **2.** Write the missing words.

best	worst

1. He wins all the races. He is the _____ athlete.

2. She was sick for a week. It was the _____ cold she

ever had.

shop	shopped	races	raced

1. I _____ at the store every day. Yesterday,

I _____ for clothes.

2. He _____ around the block everyday. Yesterday, he

_____ around the block five times.

go	going	play	playing

1. I _____ to Jefferson school this year. Next year,

I am _____ to Davis school.

2. The Tigers are _____ the Hornets tomorrow. They

_____ every year.

THE MARBLE CHAMP pp. 256A–273P

Written by Gary Soto   Illustrated by Ken Spengler

BUILD BACKGROUND FOR LANGUAGE SUPPORT

I. FOCUS ON READING

Focus on Skills

Develop Visual Literacy

OBJECTIVE: Identify steps in a process

TPR

Ask students if they have ever taken a picture with a camera. Demonstrate taking a picture with a camera, a Polaroid camera, if possible. Explain each step as you do it. For example: *First, I turn the camera on by doing this. Second, I wait for this light to turn on so I know the flash is ready. Next, I focus on the picture I want to take. Then, I push this button. Finally, I pull the picture out.* Explain to students that you learned how to take a picture by learning the steps involved in the process. Turn students' attention to the photograph on p. 256. Ask students what they see in the photograph. Encourage them to use familiar vocabulary or gestures to point out the parts of the landscape, the cars, and the metal parts. Supply additional vocabulary as needed. Help students recognize that the junk materials have been arranged in positions they would not have naturally been in. Discuss how an artist might go through the steps of making a sculpture like the ones shown on the page. Ask: *What do you think happened first? Then what happened?* Have students pantomime the act of creating one of these sculptures or another similar object. Encourage them to work cooperatively on the sculpture, describing aloud the steps they are completing.

II. READ THE LITERATURE

Vocabulary

VOCABULARY
accurate
elementary
onlookers
glory
division
congratulated

Print the vocabulary words on the chalkboard. Read aloud the appropriate story sentences and emphasize any context clues. Invite students to guess what the words might mean, and note their suggestions on the board. Come to a consensus on the definition that seems right. Display a photo of a school athletic event. Help students dramatize the scene, stopping to highlight each vocabulary word as it applies to the scene: an accurate throw; the excitement of onlookers; winning the elementary division; and so on. Finally, check comprehension by reading these sentences without the underlined words. Have students check the posted word definitions and supply the correct vocabulary word.

elementary: She loved learning and could not wait to start elementary school.

congratulated: She was congratulated by her parents for working so hard.

accurate: Her aim was accurate, so the marble went in just the right direction.

glory: She watched as another player won all the glory.

onlookers: The onlookers yelled their support to the players.

division: In the girls' division, Lupe is the best player ever.

CONCEPT
training to be the best

Evaluate Prior Knowledge

Name a sports figure, and if possible, display a picture. Talk about what makes her or him good. For example, explain that a baseball player is good at hitting the ball. Mime the actions as you talk about them. Ask how the player became good. Help students conclude that athletes became good by practicing (batting) every day. Use pantomime to explain that many athletes practice every day to train. Ask why students think athletes practice so hard. Then model for students a sport or activity that you want to become better at. For example, say: *I like to run. I run early in the morning every day. I couldn't run very far at first. Now I can run far.* Ask: *What would you like to be good at?*

TPR

Develop Oral Language

Encourage students to pantomime or describe an activity they would like to become good at or one they enjoy now. They can take turns making their presentations before the whole group.

nonverbal prompt for active participation

• Preproduction: *Show us* (point to class and self) *something you like to do.*

one- or two-word response prompt

• Early production: *What do you like to do? Do you do it every day? every week? Is it easy or hard to do?* (Use pantomime to model degrees of effort.)

prompt for short answers to higher-level thinking skills

• Speech emergence: *What do you want to become good at? Do you do it now? What part of it seems hard to you?*

prompt for detailed answers to higher-level thinking skills

• Intermediate fluency: *Why do you want to become good at (activity)? What do you have to do to become good at it? What are you doing now?*

Guided Instruction

Preview and Predict

Prompt students to give or show some examples of sports that are played at school. Tell them that this story is about a good student named Lupe who is not good at sports. Say: *Lupe is not a good athlete. What makes someone a good athlete?* Display the title page of the story and ask what sport they think Lupe is about to try. Ask: *Have you ever played marbles? What do you have to do to win a marble game?* Invite some students to demonstrate with real marbles.

Then pair English-speaking students with those needing additional support. Have pairs preview the story by looking at the illustrations. Use questions to encourage predictions and reinforce the concept of training to be the best: *Which marble do you like the best? What do you have to do to be good at marbles? Are you good at marbles? Do you think Lupe will become good at marbles? Why do you think so? What would you do to practice? What do you think happens at the marble contest?*

GRAPHIC ORGANIZER
Blackline Master 41

Objectives

• To identify steps in a process
• To support hands-on learning
• To reinforce working together cooperatively

Materials

One copy of Blackline Master 41 per student; pencils; colored pencils or markers

Go over the worksheet with students. Explain that *The Marble Champ* tells about how Lupe trains to be a champion at marbles. Tell students that as they read they will record the steps that Lupe takes in the boxes on the worksheet. Emphasize that it is important to list these steps in the order that Lupe does them. For example, after reading page 261, we understand that Lupe finds some marbles and begins to practice. Model recording this step in the first box on the worksheet. You may wish to have students work together to identify steps. Students needing additional language support can point to the pictures or text which show another step, while another student records the answer on the chart. Or students can draw pictures of the steps, according to their language abilities. Reinforce the skill of identifying steps in a process. Have students use their charts or pictures to retell the story to one another.

III. BUILD SKILLS

Comprehension

REVIEW STEPS IN A PROCESS
Blackline Master 42

Objectives
• To identify steps in a process
• To recall story events
• To practice following directions

Materials
One copy of Blackline Master 42 per student; pencils; colored pencils or markers

Review the page and the directions with students. Point to Lupe at the top of the page. Help students read the text under the top picture. Repeat this process with the picture at the bottom of the page. Ask: *How did Lupe become the champ?* (She beat other marble players.) Tell students that the picture at the top shows what happened first and the one at the bottom shows what happened last. Direct students to number the other pictures on the page in the order in which they happened. Then, work together as a class to write a caption for each picture.

INFORMAL ASSESSMENT

Have students reread the first two paragraphs on p. 265. Then ask students to retell, in their own words, the order of events on the morning of the championship.

Comprehension

INTRODUCE SUMMARIZE
Blackline Master 43

Objectives
• To identify main events of a story
• To practice summarizing events
• To reinforce cooperative learning

Materials
One copy of Blackline Master 43 per student; pencils

Display the worksheet and explain that each picture shows something that happened in the story. Review the directions, explaining that an important part of a story is one that readers need to hear to understand the story. Tell students that two of the pictures show story parts that are not important. Have students circle the six pictures which show important story events. Then have students meet in small groups and use the uncompleted worksheets to summarize the story for one another.

INFORMAL ASSESSMENT

Together, reread pages 265–267. Have students summarize the scene and identify its important story parts.

Vocabulary Strategy

INTRODUCE MULTIPLE-MEANING WORDS
Blackline Master 44

Objectives
• To identify words with multiple meanings
• To support hands-on learning

Materials

One copy of Blackline Master 44 per student; pencils; scissors; blank paper; paste or glue

Go over the worksheet with students. Explain to students that each sentence contains a word that has more than one meaning. Have students with intermediate fluency read the sentences aloud. After they read each sentence, have students match the sentence to one of the pictures on the page. After students label each picture with a sentence number, have them complete steps 4 and 5. Model, if necessary, how to match the two related pictures. Urge students to paste the picture pairs side by side on the blank paper and then write the shared word below. Encourage students to use the words *beat, block, diamond,* and *marble* in original sentences.

INFORMAL ASSESSMENT

Have students reread the first sentence on p. 260, looking for words that have more than one meaning. Point out the word *bee*. Ask students what other meaning this word has and to use it in a sentence. (For example: A bee flew in the window.)

Steps in a Process

```

```



```

```



```

```

Language Support / Blackline Master 41 • **The Marble Champ 85**

How Lupe Became a Champ

1. Show how Lupe became the marble champ. **2.** Write a number next to each picture in the order they happened . **3.** Start with the Number 1.

Lupe heads for her last match.

Lupe becomes the champ.

The Whole Story

1. Find the six important parts of the story. **2.** Draw a circle around each one. **3.** Tell the story to your classmates.

 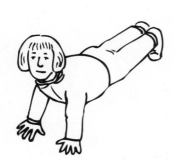 

Two Meanings for Each Word

1. Look at each picture carefully. **2.** Read the sentences below and match each sentence to a picture. **3.** Write the number of the matching sentence in the picture. **4.** Cut out the pictures. **5.** Find the two pictures that use the same word but have different meanings.

1. No one played on the baseball diamond.
2. The baby threw a block.
3. She beat the eggs.
4. My mother has a diamond ring.
5. She shot the marble.
6. She beat all the other players.
7. The steps are made of marble.
8. I like to walk around my block.

a. _____   b. _____   c. _____   d. _____

e. _____   f. _____   g. _____   h. _____

THE PAPER DRAGON pp. 274A–307P

Written by Marguerite W. Davol Illustrated by Robert Sabuda

BUILD BACKGROUND FOR LANGUAGE SUPPORT

I. FOCUS ON READING

Focus on Skills

Develop Visual Literacy

OBJECTIVE: Identify sequence of events

TPR

Direct students' attention to the picture on page 274 in their books and ask them what they see. Encourage them to use any words they know to identify colors and objects in the picture. Have them point to objects and colors as you name them. Then have volunteers come to the front of the class to point to and name objects in the picture. Discuss what the girl is doing. Ask questions such as: *Did she just start writing? How do you know this? Do you think this is a hard letter for her to write? What makes you think so? How do you think she feels?* Then encourage volunteers to help you make up a story about the painting. Start by giving each student some letter paper and a pencil. Show a letter to clarify the goal. Have students act out the painting. As one student discards a crumpled letter, have the next begin another version. At each turnover, ask students what they think might happen next. Invite volunteers to suggest, verbally or with drawing, what the letter's topic might be.

II. READ THE LITERATURE

Vocabulary

VOCABULARY
uprooted
scorched
heroic
billowed
devour
quench

Display the picture of the dragon on pages 286–287. Help students dramatize an interaction between a dragon and a human. As the students formulate sentences for their characters write them on the board, continuing until there is a complete dialogue of the skit they will perform. Have one group perform the skit. Then incorporate the vocabulary words into the skit and write them on the board in place of other words the students might have used. You can help them prepare by asking them questions related to the vocabulary words:

scorched: What happened when the fire from the dragon's mouth and nose touched trees and houses? Did it burn them up? Did it turn them brown? The fire <u>scorched</u> the trees.

billowed: Look at the smoke. After the flames, big clouds of smoke <u>billowed</u> out of the dragon's nose. Use circular movements of your cupped hands to suggest billowing clouds.

quench: We must put out the dragon's fire. Quick! Get some water. We will use it to <u>quench</u> the dragon's fire.

uprooted: The dragon is waving its tail madly. Now there is a big windstorm! If we don't stop the dragon, the trees will be <u>uprooted</u> by the wind.

devour: Watch out! That mean dragon is really mad now. It wants to <u>devour</u> us for breakfast.

heroic: You stopped the dragon. You are a very brave person who faced danger to save us. Have you done other <u>heroic</u> things?

After students understand the words, invite them to tell stories about other heroic deeds they know about. Urge them to use as many vocabulary words as they can.

CONCEPT
forms of communication

Evaluate Prior Knowledge

Direct students again to the visual literacy painting on page 275. Remind them that the artist who painted this young girl tried to tell a story. Telling a story with pictures is one form of communication. Point out objects in the classroom that are forms of communication: books, signs, pictures, the clock. As you point out each, ask students: *What does this tell you?* Help them figure out the answers. Then explain that people can communicate with their faces and bodies. Point out or model a facial expression or body posture. Tell them to watch you and think about what you are saying. You might show or point out: *I'm astonished* or *I don't want to talk to anyone.* Ask: *What do you think I'm telling you?* Now present one of these messages in both written and visual forms.

TPR

Develop Oral Language

Invite students to work in groups to experiment with different forms of communication. Give, or allow groups to choose, simple messages. Have groups present the messages in written, visual, and kinesthetic forms, with these tasks spread among students of varying fluency.

nonverbal prompt for active participation

• Preproduction: *Show us* (point to self and class) *your message. I think it says* (insert message). *Am I right? Model using gesture to indicate "yes" or "no"."*

one- or two-word response prompt

• Early production: *Does your message say* (insert message)*? Can you say any part of your message with words? Can you show us the message with your body?*

prompt for short answers to higher-level thinking skills

• Speech emergence: *How is your message different in this form than in the other forms your group showed? How is it the same?*

prompt for detailed answers to higher-level thinking skills

• Intermediate fluency: *What is your message? Which form do you think works best to communicate this message? Why?*

Guided Instruction

Preview and Predict

Remind students that they know that this story features a dragon. As they view the title page, ask students whether they think it will be a mean or a friendly dragon. Have students page through the story with you, discussing the illustrations, the story setting, and the folktale genre, and reinforcing the concept of forms of communication. Point out Mi Fei. Ask questions such as: *What is Mi Fei painting? What could this painting's story be? Why do you think this man looks the way he does? What are some good things to do if a dragon is coming? What would you do if you lived in that village? What do you think Mi Fei is going to do? How do you think he feels about meeting the dragon? Why? How would you describe this dragon? Do you think that Mi Fei will fight the dragon? What do you think he will do?*

GRAPHIC ORGANIZER
Blackline Master 45

Objectives

• To reinforce sequence of events
• To practice summarizing
• To reinforce working together cooperatively

Materials

One copy of Blackline Master 45 per student; pencils; colored pencils or markers

Explain to students that they will use the worksheet to record important events that happen in the story. Tell students that it is important to list these events in the order that they happen. Then work together to look through the story and talk about important events. As the class picks out important events, write them on the chalkboard. Then have the class choose six. Have more fluent students write appropriate phrases or sentences in the chart. Less fluent students can draw pictures of the events. Encourage those who drew pictures to write captions, if they're able to do so.

Reinforce the skill of identifying sequence. Have students use their charts or drawings to retell the story to one another.

III. BUILD SKILLS

Comprehension

REVIEW SEQUENCE OF EVENTS
Blackline Master 46

Objectives
- To practice putting events in sequence
- To provide hands-on experience
- To follow directions

Materials

One copy of Blackline Master 46 per student; scissors; paste or glue; newsprint; pencils

Go over the page with students. Explain that the pictures show things that happened in the first part of the story. Discuss the pictures and read the directions at the bottom of the page together. Have students cut out the pictures and paste them in sequence on a long strip of newsprint, leaving space to write below each picture. More fluent students can write one or two sentences to tell what is happening. Less fluent students may write words or phrases that tell about the pictures. When they are done, partners can use the pictures to retell this part of the story.

INFORMAL ASSESSMENT Show students the story illustrations on pages 282 and 286–287. Ask them to tell which event occurred first.

Comprehension

REVIEW SUMMARIZE
Blackline Master 47

Objectives
- To summarize a story
- To provide hands-on experience
- To work together cooperatively

Materials

One copy of Blackline Master 47 per small group; colored pencils or markers; scissors; paste or glue; craft sticks

Have students meet in small groups to color the pictures and review the directions. Model how to cut out each picture and paste it to a craft stick to make a puppet. Invite groups to use the puppets to tell the most important things that happen in the story. Remind them that not every event in the story is important.

INFORMAL ASSESSMENT Help students read aloud the second paragraph on page 281. Then prompt them to summarize the paragraph without giving every detail. Choose other paragraphs or portions of the story for them to read and summarize, such as the text on page 292.

Vocabulary Strategy

INTRODUCE FIGURATIVE LANGUAGE
Blackline Master 48

Objectives
- To recognize figurative language
- To interpret figurative language

Materials

One copy of Blackline Master 48 per student; pencils; colored pencils or markers (optional)

Have students discuss the pictures, describing what they see. Point out the phrases and explain that each tells about one of the pictures. Emphasize that the phrases don't actually name the pictured thing. Read the directions aloud, and model the first item. More fluent speakers can work independently and share their responses afterward. Less fluent speakers can complete the activity with partners or in a group. After students have finished, discuss how they made their choices.

INFORMAL ASSESSMENT

Have students leaf through the story illustrations. Prompt them to create figurative phrases to describe items they see in the pictures. For example, a horse could be "lightning on four legs."

Sequence of Events

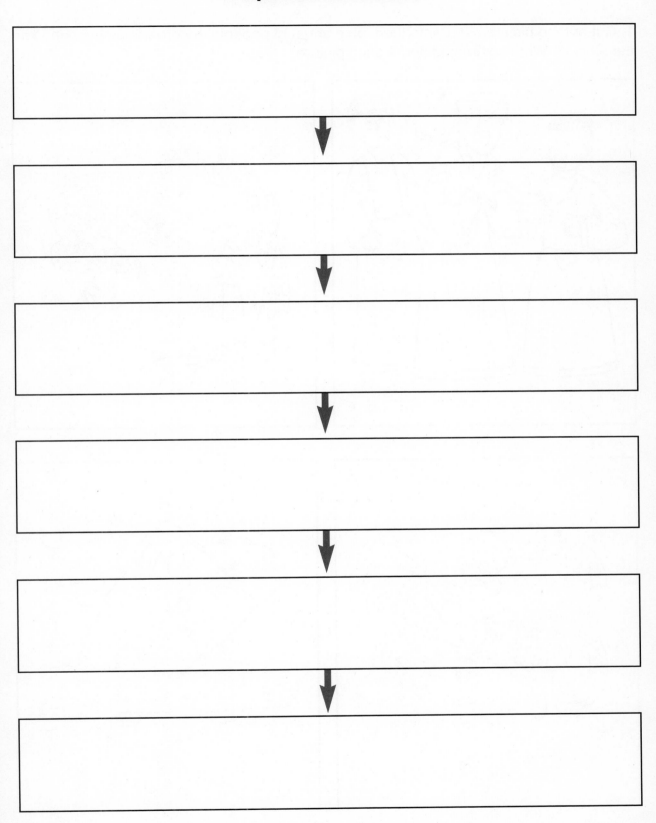

Here is a Start

1. Cut out the pictures. **2.** Paste them on a sheet of paper in the order they happened in the story. **3.** Write something about each picture.

A Short Story

1. Cut out each picture. **2.** Paste it to a stick. **3.** Use the pictures to tell what happens in the story.

What Could It Mean?

1. Match the words to the pictures below. **2.** Write the words below the picture.

1. a door to other worlds
2. wind captured in paper
3. flying music

4. a dragon with one big eye
5. balls of cotton
6. fire wrapped in paper

_____

_____

_____

_____

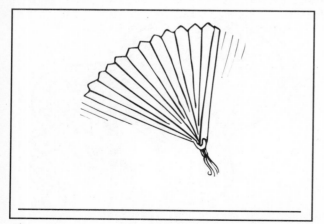

_____

_____

Grade 5

GRANDMA ESSIE'S COVERED WAGON pp. 308A–339P

Written by David Williams Illustrated by Wiktor Sadowski

BUILD BACKGROUND FOR LANGUAGE SUPPORT

I. FOCUS ON READING

Focus on Skills

OBJECTIVE: Identify steps in a process

TPR

Develop Visual Literacy

Pantomime for students a simple process, such as making a sandwich. As you pantomime, prompt students to understand the steps involved by holding up fingers and saying: *First, do this. Second, do this.*, etc. Then gather students in small groups and assign them a simple task, such as wrapping a present, tying a knot, etc. Have students work together to figure out the steps they must take in order to do the task. Then have each group show the rest of the class the steps involved in completing the task. Ask students: *Is there another order in which these steps could be completed?* Explain to students that many stories also contain a process, or an order of events, which lead the characters into different situations. Then have students look at the picture on page 308 and comment on it. Offer vocabulary, or prompt students with questions about specific elements: *Show me a horse. Where is the girl? Point to all the people. Can you find a house?* Ask students to consider which person got on the horse first. Say: *Who do you think was the first person on the horse?* Encourage students to make up a story about the picture. If necessary, suggest a beginning such as: *One day a knight was riding a horse through some trees.* Invite volunteers to mime the actions as they are described. Whenever students suggest a line of action, have the acting volunteers show it. Use clue words such as *first*, *next*, and *then* to emphasize sequence. Finally, tell students that they are going to make a painting like this one. Ask: *What would you do first?* Again, invite volunteers to dramatize how they would make a painting. What would they do first, next, and last?

II. READ THE LITERATURE

VOCABULARY
bashful
canvas
granite
orphanage
tornado
cemetery

Vocabulary

Print the vocabulary words on the chalkboard and on index cards for each student. Use illustrations and pantomiming to introduce the words:

bashful: Have a volunteer say hello to you and act <u>bashful</u> in response. Ask students to repeat the aspects of the volunteer's behavior that makes her or him *bashful*. Ask students if a <u>bashful</u> person is bold or shy around people.

canvas: Show students the picture on page 313, and then pass around a piece of <u>canvas</u>. Point to the wagon top and explain that it is made of <u>canvas</u>.

granite: Display color photographs of the mineral <u>granite</u> and of graniteware (look in books about collectibles). If possible, allow students to handle a piece of <u>granite</u> from your landscape or a rock collection. Relate the pictures to the cooking utensils shown on page 315.

orphanage: Group students in families. Remove the "mother" and "father." Explain that now the "children" are orphans—they have no mothers or fathers. Direct orphaned students to a part of the room decorated with the picture of a house. Say: *This is the <u>orphanage</u> where the orphans live together.*

tornado: Have students turn to the picture on page 318 and point out the <u>tornado</u>. Invite students to act out a <u>tornado</u> or its effects.

cemetery: Point out the <u>cemetery</u> on page 329, and ask students what kind of place it is. Prompt them to tell what they know about cemeteries.

Then have students form small groups and give each group a vocabulary word. Have students look through magazines for pictures that illustrate the word. Tell students that each group must write a sentence using the vocabulary word and relating it to the picture. Have groups take turns presenting their sentences and pictures to the rest of the class.

Evaluate Prior Knowledge

CONCEPT
biography

Display biographies of some people students are familiar with, preferably ones that have the subject's picture on the cover. Explain that the books tell about real people, such as American patriots, athletes, and musicians. Hold up the books one at a time, and have students try to name the subject and tell anything they know about the person. Explain that these books have been written just to tell about the person's life. Hold up the book and say: *It tells many things. It tells when (she/he) was born. It tells where (she/he) was born. It tells the name of (her/his) school. It tells what (she/he) liked to do.* Invite students to name other things that could be in the book. Explain that these books are biographies, or books that tell the true story of a person's life. Ask students: *What things would be in a biography about you? Show or tell us three things about your life that you think readers would want to know.*

Develop Oral Language

Prompt students to demonstrate or talk about some things that might be in books written about them. Have available a map on which they might point out a birthplace.

nonverbal prompt for active participation

• Preproduction: *When and where were you born?* Model and have students write their ages on the chalkboard, along with their dates of birth. *Show us* (point to self and class and model with fingers) *how many are in your family. Show us* (indicate pantomime) *an activity you like to do.*

one- or two-word response prompt

• Early production: *What is your birthday? Where were you born? Is this where you were born?* (Point out their birthplaces on the map.) *What are you showing us now? It looks like* (indicate demonstrated activity). *Would you put this in a biography?*

prompt for short answers to higher-level thinking skills

• Speech emergence: *What do you think should be in your biography? Who is in your family? Where do you live now? What is one of your favorite things to do?*

prompt for detailed answers to higher-level thinking skills

• Intermediate fluency: *Tell us about the things that would be in a book about you. Why would you choose these things to include? What do they tell about you?*

Guided Instruction

Preview and Predict

Have students look at the picture on page 310. Ask students: *When do you think this story takes place? Why?* Then explain to students that the author writes about his grandmother and her real-life experiences as a little girl. Clarify that the selection is made of many little stories. Invite students to page through the story illustrations, prompting discussion and reinforcing the concept of biographies. Ask questions such as: *Who do you think this little girl is? Where do you think this family might be going? When do you think this story happens? How do you know that? How do you think the little girl feels now? Have you ever felt this way? Why do you think the family is sitting around a fire? Tell about a time when you ate outdoors like this.* After students preview the illustrations, encourage them to read to confirm or adjust their predictions.

GRAPHIC ORGANIZER
Blackline Master 49

Objectives
- To review steps in a process
- To relate steps in a process to story events
- To encourage cooperative learning

Materials
One copy of Blackline Master 49 per student; pencils; colored pencils or markers

Explain to students that *Grandma Essie's Covered Wagon* is the story of the author's grandmother's life. They will use this process chart to remember key events in the main character's life. Explain that the boxes are for the steps that Essie and her family take as they move around to different locations. Remind students that they should always list steps in the order that they happen. Then ask students to name or show in an illustration the first place Essie's family goes. Have students with more fluent language skills list this place in the chart. Students needing language support can draw pictures of each place. Then work with fluent partners to create captions for the pictures.

Reinforce the skill of identifying steps in a process. Have students use their charts or pictures to create cartoon or storyboard versions of the selection.

III. BUILD SKILLS
Comprehension

REVIEW STEPS IN A PROCESS
Blackline Master 50

Objectives
- To review steps in a process
- To support hands-on learning
- To practice following directions

Materials
One copy of Blackline Master 50 per student; scissors; paste or glue; newsprint; pencils

Tell students that long ago nothing was wasted and that if a dress could no longer be worn it might be made into a quilt. Clarify what a quilt is. Explain that the pictures show this process but that the steps are not in the right order. Read the directions together. Have students cut out the pictures and arrange them in the correct order. They can paste the pictures in a row on newsprint and connect them with arrows. Ask students to then draw what they think might happen next. Then help students write a few words or a sentence to tell about each picture. Have students discuss the steps involved in the process of making a quilt and pantomime the steps taken.

INFORMAL ASSESSMENT
Have students look at page 315. Ask them to think about and describe the steps in processes such as building a fire, making a stew, or camping for the night.

Comprehension

REVIEW SEQUENCE OF EVENTS
Blackline Master 51

Objectives
- To review sequence of events
- To encourage critical thinking

Materials

One copy of Blackline Master 51 per student; pencils; colored pencils or markers (optional)

Discuss the pictures on the worksheet with the students and help them read the captions below each one. Explain that the pictures represent a sequence of events that take place when a tornado hits. Tell students that the first picture shows the first thing that happened, but the other pictures are not in the correct order. Have students draw a line from the first picture to the picture that shows what happened next. Then have them draw a line to the picture that shows what happened after that. Have students tell how they would respond to a tornado, using words from the story, their captions, and pantomime.

INFORMAL ASSESSMENT

To assess students' understanding of sequence of events, have them reread pages 326-328. Then ask them to describe the order of events which led to Stella's death.

Vocabulary Strategy

REVIEW FIGURATIVE LANGUAGE
Blackline Master 52

Objectives

• To review figurative language
• To encourage the use of picture clues

Materials

One copy of Blackline Master 52 per student; pencils

Go over the page with students, asking them what they see in the pictures. Read the phrases at the top of the page, and explain that each phrase describes something in one of the pictures. Clarify that the words do not actually name the objects, but instead tell what they are like. You may model how to write the words at the bottom of a picture. Pair students according to their fluency, allowing more fluent students to complete their work independently and then assist less fluent students.

INFORMAL ASSESSMENT

Have students look at illustrations from the story. Point out objects in the pictures and ask: *What does this make you think of? What is this like?* Work together to create figurative language about the objects.

Name_____ Date_____

Steps in a Process

```
┌─────────────────────────────────────────────────┐
│                                                 │
│                                                 │
└─────────────────────────────────────────────────┘
                        ↓
┌─────────────────────────────────────────────────┐
│                                                 │
│                                                 │
└─────────────────────────────────────────────────┘
                        ↓
┌─────────────────────────────────────────────────┐
│                                                 │
│                                                 │
└─────────────────────────────────────────────────┘
                        ↓
┌─────────────────────────────────────────────────┐
│                                                 │
│                                                 │
└─────────────────────────────────────────────────┘
                        ↓
┌─────────────────────────────────────────────────┐
│                                                 │
│                                                 │
└─────────────────────────────────────────────────┘
                        ↓
┌─────────────────────────────────────────────────┐
│                                                 │
│                                                 │
└─────────────────────────────────────────────────┘
                        ↓
┌─────────────────────────────────────────────────┐
│                                                 │
│                                                 │
└─────────────────────────────────────────────────┘
```

From Dress to Quilt

1. Cut out the four pictures. **2.** Put them in the right order. **3.** Paste them on a sheet of paper. **4.** Draw what might happen next in the empty box.

How Did It Happen?

1. Look at the pictures and read the sentences. **2.** The first picture shows what happened first. **3.** Draw a line to the picture that shows what happened next. **4.** Then draw a line to the next picture. **5.** Do this until you come to the last picture.

She was playing
under the tree.

She saw a tornado
coming.

They climbed out
of the cellar.

They hid from the
storm in the cellar.

The family climbed
down into the cellar.

The storm had
torn up the tree.

What Do You See?

1. Find the words that help to describe a picture. **2.** Write the words in the space below the picture.

1. a silver ribbon	**3.** a metal forest
2. dry as a desert	**4.** flat as a pancake

GOING BACK HOME pp. 340A–371P

Written by Toyomi Igus Illustrated by Michelle Wood

BUILD BACKGROUND FOR LANGUAGE SUPPORT

I. FOCUS ON READING

Focus on Skills

Develop Visual Literacy

OBJECTIVE: Identify author's purpose and point of view

TPR

Have students look at the picture *The Storyteller*. Have students count out the number of people in the picture. Then have volunteers reproduce the poses shown in the picture. Have students look at the picture and point to the person they represent. Then ask: *Who are you looking at?* Guide students to see that everyone in the picture is focused on the largest figure. Point out the title of the picture and read it aloud. Ask students: *Who is the storyteller?* Encourage other students to take the places of those in the circle. Then ask: *Who is the most important person in the picture? What makes you think so?* Then ask others to show where they think the artist stood or sat to get this view of the scene. Explain, with modeling if necessary, that the artist wants us to feel as if we are sitting in the circle around the storyteller. Brainstorm with students what the storyteller might be saying. Introduce the idea that he might be telling a story about events from long ago. Have students take turns playing the storyteller and audience. Encourage the audience to ask the storyteller questions or to help tell a familiar story.

II. READ THE LITERATURE

Vocabulary

VOCABULARY
heritage
livestock
influenced
thrive
survival
tiresome

Print the vocabulary words on the chalkboard. Put students in small groups and have each group take one word from the list. Explain to students that they may look through magazines and encyclopedias to choose pictures which may represent the word, or they may choose to role-play the vocabulary word. You may want to give students suggestions if they are having trouble, for example: pictures of people from different cultures to show *heritage*; pictures of farm animals for *livestock*; showing examples of successful gardens or healthy animals for *thrive*; role-playing changing another person's behavior or attitudes for *influenced*; and showing pictures of or dramatizing people coping with adverse weather and terrain for *survival*. Have each group present their word to the class.

Read the pertinent story sentences, and encourage students to guess what each word might mean. Record their suggestions on the board. Paraphrase each sentence, using students' suggestions. Discuss which suggestion seems most likely. Finally, give students dictionary definitions to check their conclusions.

Evaluate Prior Knowledge

CONCEPT
artistic expression

Display different photographs or paintings of various artwork. Or point to artwork which may already be displayed in the classroom. Explain that each piece of artwork is different because each was created by a different individual. Then ask students to draw a picture of a flower. Have volunteers display their pictures. Ask students: *Are these pictures the same or different?* Encourage students to explain why they chose the colors they used, or what type of flower they drew, and why. Point out that each student expressed themselves differently. Then have students look at magazines and art books and ask them to find a picture representing family life. Display several pictures for the class and have them compare and contrast the people and objects in each picture. Encourage students to think about where the people may have lived and in what time they lived.

TPR

nonverbal prompt for active participation

one- or two-word response prompt

prompt for short answers to higher-level thinking skills

prompt for detailed answers to higher-level thinking skills

Develop Oral Language

• Preproduction: *Can you point to all the people in this picture? Is this the same number of people in your family?*

• Early production: *Point to the picture you like the most. Do you think the artist who drew or took this picture is from the same time as we are today?*

• Speech emergence: *Point to the picture which most resembles your family. What is similar about this family and yours? Point to the picture which seems most opposite from your family. Why?*

• Intermediate fluency: *Do you think the artists who created these pictures or took these photographs were part of the family? Why or why not? What do you think the artist felt about the family? What feeling do you think the artist was trying to express?*

Guided Instruction

Preview and Predict

Highlight the illustration on the title page. Point out Michelle Wood on page 342, and read aloud the biographical note about her. Explain that this selection tells true information about life long ago. Preview the selection together through discussion of the illustrations. Ask: *Do you think this picture shows something that happened in the last few years or something that happened long ago? Why? How is the clothing the same as or different from yours? How do you think these people know one another? Do these people remind you of anyone in your own family? Who are they like? What does the house tell you about the people who live there?* Encourage students to make additional predictions as they read, and then discuss how accurate their predictions were.

GRAPHIC ORGANIZER
Blackline Master 53

Objectives

• To understand author's purpose and point of view
• To support hands-on learning
• To reinforce working together cooperatively

Materials

One copy of Blackline Master 53 per student; pencils; colored pencils or markers

Explain to students that this story was created by an artist and an author, who expressed in writing what the artist drew. Review the worksheet with students. Explain that using it will help them answer the questions: *Why did the author write this story? Why did the artist create these paintings?* Tell students that as they read the story, they will fill in the chart with answers to these questions based on what they learn. Prompt students with statements such as : *I think she wrote this story to tell us _____. I think the artist made this painting to make us _____. I think she wants us to _____.*
I think she tells the story through _____ eyes. Reread the biographical notes on p. 342 and ask students: *What are these paintings about?* (They are about the artist's search for her family history.) Model recording the answer on the chart. If necessary, students can draw pictures and then tell about or show them. For example, they might draw a picture of the slave family and say that the author wrote to tell us about the old days. Invite students to show how the artist feels about her family and to record this in their charts, using words or pictures.

Reinforce the skill of recognizing author's point of view. Read aloud the first story sentence, emphasizing the word *I*. Ask students whose point of view the story is told from.

III. BUILD SKILLS

Comprehension

REVIEW AUTHOR'S PURPOSE, POINT OF VIEW
Blackline Master 54

Objectives
- To review author's purpose
- To review point of view
- To practice following directions

Materials
One copy of Blackline Master 54 per student; pencils

Before beginning the worksheet, review with students some of the reasons writers write. Read the directions with students. Then have a volunteer read aloud the first sentence. Ask: *Do you think Michelle Wood would say this about Going Back Home?* Say: *If you do, mark the box labeled* Yes. *If not, mark the box labeled* No. Some students will benefit from working with partners or completing the activity as a group. Discuss other comments Michelle Wood might make about her story.

INFORMAL ASSESSMENT

To assess their comprehension of author's purpose, have students reread page 347. Then ask: *Why did Michelle Wood include an African American soldier in this picture?* Discuss students' answers as a class.

Comprehension

REVIEW SUMMARIZE
Blackline Master 55

Objectives
- To summarize information
- To recall information from reading
- To reinforce hands-on learning

Materials
One copy of Blackline Master 55 per student; pencils; scissors; paste or glue; newsprint

Remind students that this story is a collaboration between an artist who created pictures and an author who wrote about them. Have students cut out each picture on the page and paste it on a page of newsprint as if they were pasting it in a photograph album. Tell students to think about what they learned as they read *Going Back Home*. Then have more students write words, phrases, or sentences that tell about each picture, according to their ability. Offer assistance as needed. You may pair native English speakers with those needing additional language support.

INFORMAL ASSESSMENT

Have students use their "photograph album" to summarize in their own words what they learned from the selection.

Vocabulary Strategy

REVIEW MULTIPLE-MEANING WORDS
Blackline Master 56

Objectives
• To review multiple-meaning words
• To use multiple-meaning words correctly
• To practice following directions

Materials
One copy of Blackline Master 56 per student; pencils

Review with students that sometimes the same word may have more than one meaning. Read aloud the directions with students. Make sure they understand that they are to use the same word to complete each pair of sentences. Have students read aloud the words at the top of the page. If necessary, model trying out words in the first incomplete sentence. You may want to read aloud the incomplete sentences. After students have completed the worksheet, have them use these four words in original sentences.

INFORMAL ASSESSMENT

Have volunteers read aloud the second paragraph on page 356. Call students' attention to the word *treat* and explain that this word has more than one meaning. Ask students to think of an example of a *treat,* as used in this sentence. Then ask students what other meaning the word *treat* has. Ask students to use *treat* in a sentence.

Point of View

**Author's Purpose and
Point of View**

Why Did She Write It?

1. Why did Michele Wood write *Going Back Home*? **2.** Read each sentence. **3.** Put a check mark next to *Yes* or *No*.

1. I want people to enjoy my art.
❑ yes   ❑ no

2. I want to share my family's history.
❑ yes   ❑ no

3. I want to make people get the hiccups.
❑ yes   ❑ no

4. I want people to learn how to grow cotton.
❑ yes   ❑ no

5. I want to tell what African Americans gave to America.
❑ yes   ❑ no

Name_____ Date_____

One Story, Many Stories

1. Cut out the pictures. **2.** Paste the pictures on a page. **3.** Write about each picture.

One In Two

1. Read the two sentences in each box. 2. Find one word that fits in both sentences.
3. Write the word on the lines.

grew	land	stories	well

1. He reads _____.

The house has three _____.

2. She runs very _____.

They got their water from a _____.

3. He _____ cotton.

She _____ up in Indiana.

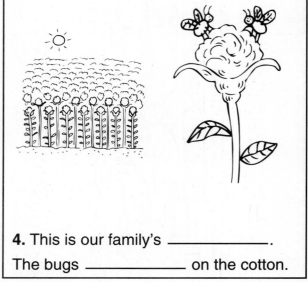

4. This is our family's _____.

The bugs _____ on the cotton.

A MOUNTAIN OF A MONUMENT pp. 372A–381P

BUILD BACKGROUND FOR LANGUAGE SUPPORT

I. FOCUS ON READING
Focus on Skills

OBJECTIVE: Identify sequence of events

TPR

Develop Visual Literacy

Tell students as they look at the sculpture on page 372, that this is one of the most famous places in the world. Find out whether anyone has seen a picture of it before. Point to Egypt on a map. Ask: *How big do you think this monument is? Why do you think so?* Encourage students to use words and body language to describe what they see. Use pictures to explain that the head is that of a person and the body is that of a lion. Invite students to point to these named parts. Then discuss whether students have changed much in their 11 years. Ask: *How have you changed?* Invite students to show or tell some ways they behaved at earlier times in their life. Explain that the monument is very old—4,500 years old! Have students tell you or show some ways it could change during those years. Ask: *What are some things that could wear away the monument?*

II. READ THE LITERATURE

VOCABULARY
sculpture
awesome
nostril
dedicate
hail
explosives

Vocabulary

Print the vocabulary words on the chalkboard, and introduce them by reading aloud the sentences in Teaching Chart 86. Have students discuss and respond physically to the photographs on pages 374–375, prompting them to use the vocabulary words in their responses. For example:

sculpture: How is this mountain different from other mountains? Do you know of any other sculpture made in the side of a mountain? Show me one way to create a sculpture.

awesome: What words would you use to talk about it? Would it fill you full of wonder? What makes it an awesome sight? Show me your face when you see an awesome sight.

explosives: How do you think this sculpture was made? Do you think it was all done with hand tools? Why not? How could someone use explosives to help move big chunks of rocks? Show me what happens when explosives are used.

nostril: Point to the horse's nose. How do you think the nostril was cut out? Show me.

dedicate: Many people took part in a ceremony to give this sculpture a very special name. Show me something you think they did to dedicate this place.

hail: There are ways to show that people are special, too. The song "Hail to the Chief" is sometimes played when the President walks in. What do you think that means?

Evaluate Prior Knowledge

CONCEPT
heroes

Display pictures of people, famous or ordinary, who might seem like heroes to students. Be sure to include people that reflect the class's ethnic and national background. Prompt students to tell or show what they know about these people. Model by naming or showing a picture of someone you think is a hero. Develop the concept that a hero is someone who does something unselfish for others, sometimes risking danger in the process. Discuss why the people in the pictures are heroes. Ask students: *Have you ever been a hero? What did you do?*

Develop Oral Language

Invite students to draw, pantomime, or tell about a time when they acted heroically. Students may prepare to speak by meeting with partners and rehearsing what they will say.

• Preproduction: *Show us* (point to self and class) *when you were a hero* (indicate pictures or pantomime). *It looks like you* (name action shown). *How did you feel when you did this?* (Model showing emotion with body language.)

• Early production: *Did you act like a hero by* (name action shown)? *Did this make you proud? How did it make you feel? How did others act toward you? Can you tell us one word about what happened?*

• Speech emergence: *What happened when you were a hero? Who did you help? When did it happen? How did you feel before this happened? How did you feel after?*

• Intermediate fluency: *What did you do to be a hero? Who helped you? Have you ever acted this way before? What made this time special? What were you thinking? How did you feel? What happened afterward?*

Guided Instruction

Preview and Predict

Have students read the headline, "Time for Kids," and explain that this selection is a news story. After students read the title, ask what they think the news story is about. Reinforce the concept of heroes as you review and discuss the illustrations. Invite students to describe what they see and make predictions. Then ask: *What questions do you have about this sculpture?* Write their questions on the chalkboard; for example: *Where is the sculpture? Why was it made? How was it made? Is it a sculpture of a real person? If it is, what was special about this person? Is the sculpture finished? Is it easy to visit?*

Ask students which questions they think the story might answer. After students have read the selection, you may wish to return to these questions.

Objectives

• To reinforce sequence of events
• To support hands-on learning
• To reinforce working together cooperatively

Materials

One copy of Blackline Master 57 per student; pencils

Remind students that they have used charts like this one before to show the order in which events took place. Explain that on this blackline master they will use the boxes to tell how the Crazy Horse Memorial was made. You may want to reproduce the chart on the chalkboard. Have students with limited writing skills draw each episode as you talk about it. Reread pages 375–376 aloud together. As you read, have students identify events in the monument's creation.

Reinforce the skill of sequence of events by having students use their charts to summarize the steps in building the monument.

III. BUILD SKILLS

Comprehension

REVIEW AUTHOR'S PURPOSE, POINT OF VIEW
Blackline Master 58

Objectives
- To identify reasons authors write
- To identify author's point of view
- To practice writing

Materials
One copy of Blackline Master 58 per student; pencils

Remind students that they know that stories and articles are written for many different reasons. Read with students the first set of directions and, if necessary, the numbered phrases. Help those with limited language fluency to select answers. Then read the second set of directions, and have students write their answers on the lines provided. You may wish to pair students with limited English with partners or allow students to draw and describe a picture.

INFORMAL ASSESSMENT

Tell students that artists also have reasons in mind when they create art. Show the sculpture on page 374, and ask students to tell what they think the artist's reasons were for creating it.

Comprehension

REVIEW MULTIPLE-MEANING WORDS
Blackline Master 59

Objectives
- To recognize that words can have more than one meaning
- To practice using multiple-meaning words correctly

Materials
One copy of Blackline Master 59 per student; pencils

Have students read aloud the words at the top of the page. Point out that each has more than one meaning. Read aloud the directions, reminding students that they have worked with sentence pairs like these before. Be sure they understand that the same word must fit in both sentences within each box. If necessary, model the first item. After students finish the worksheet, ask them to use these four words in original sentences.

INFORMAL ASSESSMENT

Have volunteers read aloud the first paragraph on page 377. Prompt students to find words with more than one meaning. (e.g., top, face, work, foot) Have them use these words to create their own sentences. Their sentences should reflect the multiple meanings of the word.

Vocabulary Strategy

Objectives
• To read figurative language
• To interpret figurative language
• To reinforce hands-on learning

Materials
One copy of Blackline Master 60 per student; pencils; colored pencils or markers

Go over the directions with students, making sure they understand that they are not to draw a balloon, a storm, or a river, but things that are like a balloon, a storm, or a river. Help them brainstorm the characteristics of each item. For example: a balloon seems to weigh nothing, floats in the air, and is easily blown by a breeze. Then have them visualize other things that have or seem to have these characteristics. (a dandelion puff, a graceful dancer, an astronaut on the moon) After students complete the worksheet, have them share and talk about their pictures.

INFORMAL ASSESSMENT
Have students look at the pictures on pages 374–377. Encourage them to describe what they see in terms of comparisons. For example, the crowd might be as noisy as _____, a horse as fast as _____, or Standing Bull as brave as _____.

Sequence of Events

```
┌─────────────────────────────────────────────────┐
│                                                 │
│                                                 │
└─────────────────────────────────────────────────┘
                        ↓
┌─────────────────────────────────────────────────┐
│                                                 │
│                                                 │
└─────────────────────────────────────────────────┘
                        ↓
┌─────────────────────────────────────────────────┐
│                                                 │
│                                                 │
└─────────────────────────────────────────────────┘
                        ↓
┌─────────────────────────────────────────────────┐
│                                                 │
│                                                 │
└─────────────────────────────────────────────────┘
                        ↓
┌─────────────────────────────────────────────────┐
│                                                 │
│                                                 │
└─────────────────────────────────────────────────┘
                        ↓
┌─────────────────────────────────────────────────┐
│                                                 │
│                                                 │
└─────────────────────────────────────────────────┘
                        ↓
┌─────────────────────────────────────────────────┐
│                                                 │
│                                                 │
└─────────────────────────────────────────────────┘
```

What Did You Get From It?

1. Read the words. **2.** Check *Right* if the words tell why "A Mountain of a Monument" was written. **3.** Check *Wrong* if the words do not tell why it was written. **4.** What do you remember best about this story? **5.** Write about it on the lines below.

1.	to tell us about the Crazy Horse statute	❑ right	❑ wrong
2.	to tell us about Ohio	❑ right	❑ wrong
3.	to tell us who Crazy Horse is	❑ right	❑ wrong
4.	to make us want to make statues	❑ right	❑ wrong
5.	to make us want to see the statue	❑ right	❑ wrong

_____

_____

_____

_____

_____

_____

_____

_____

_____

_____

Name_____ Date_____

Two Views of a Word

1. Read the two sentences in each picture box. **2.** Find a word that fits in both. **3.** Write the word on the lines.

head	rocks	pays	view

1. There are _____ in the path.

She _____ the baby.

2. They _____ the mountain.

The _____ is wonderful.

3. The _____ is carved on the side of the mountain.

She is the _____ of the museum.

4. The family _____ a visit to the park.

He _____ for the tickets.

Name_____ Date_____

Draw It

1. Draw something that is as light as a balloon.

_____

2. Draw something that sounds like thunder.

_____

3. Draw a river of light.

CARLOS AND THE SKUNK pp. 366A–407P

Written by Jan Romero Stevens Illustrated by Jeanne Arnold

BUILD BACKGROUND FOR LANGUAGE SUPPORT

I. FOCUS ON READING

Focus on Skills

OBJECTIVE: Identify judgments and decisions

TPR

Develop Visual Literacy

Have students look at the picture *The Human Condition, II* by René Magritte and describe what they see. Introduce words such as *painting, easel,* and *seascape* by pointing to the items in the picture while naming them. Ask students: *Do you like to go to the sea? Do you like to paint or draw? Have you ever painted or drawn a picture of the time you spent at the sea?* Then invite students to indicate with words or gestures what is unusual about this picture. (It's a painting of a painting. The sea and the painting run into one another.) Ask: *Does this picture make you think of real life? Raise your hands for yes. Or does it make you think of a dream? Raise your hands for yes. Why?* Then say: *We don't know what the artist was thinking as he painted, but we can guess. Why do you think the artist decided to show these things in his picture?* Finally, discuss students' judgments about the painting. Explain that a judgment is like an opinion. Model how to vote "yes" or "no" about whether you like the picture. Give reasons for your choice. Then poll students for their opinions.

II. READ THE LITERATURE

Vocabulary

VOCABULARY
tortillas
peculiar
unpleasant
unbearable
stunned
nestled

Vocabulary

Print each vocabulary word on a flashcard. Display the flashcard for a word as you say it aloud and read the corresponding sentences from Teacher Chart 92. Ask students to define each word and tell what clues helped them understand it. Invite them to act out word meaning or context clues to demonstrate their understanding. Ask questions to prompt the discussion and role-play:

tortilla: Do you think a <u>tortilla</u> is a vegetable or a food like bread? Why?

nestled: Show us how you would nestle something in your hands. What do you think a village <u>nestled</u> in the mountains would look like?

stunned: Show us how Ron acted when he was <u>stunned</u>. What is another word that means the same thing as <u>stunned</u>?

unbearable: Do you think an <u>unbearable</u> smell is a nice smell or a bad smell? What does your face look like when you smell an <u>unbearable</u> smell?

unpleasant: What type of weather is <u>unpleasant</u>? What is a word that means the opposite of <u>unpleasant</u>? Show us what you think <u>unpleasant</u> weather is.

peculiar: If something is <u>peculiar</u>, is it odd or is it common? How do you look when you see something <u>peculiar</u>?

Evaluate Prior Knowledge

CONCEPT
learning

Point to the classroom of students and ask: *What are you doing here?* Point to yourself and say *What do I do here?* Encourage students to brainstorm different concepts of learning by drawing a picture of a school with your classroom in it. Ask students: *Why do you go to school?* Write their responses on the board in a word web. Explain that learning is the process of understanding information. Then put students in small groups and have them interview each other with questions such as: *What did you learn in school today? Can you show me something you learned recently?* Have students pantomime something they have recently learned, whether in school or elsewhere. Ask them to show the process—the first step in learning, the second, and so on. Model by pantomiming the process of learning how to make a sandwich. Show the steps and the mistakes a beginner might make. Question students about their pantomimes.

Develop Oral Language

nonverbal prompt for active participation

- Preproduction: *Raise your hand if the process you are showing is* (name process shown). *Was it hard to learn?* (model shaking head or nodding for no or yes) *Did you like learning it?*

one- or two-word response prompt

- Early production: *Did it take you a long time to learn* (name process shown)*? Can you tell us one thing about learning* (name process shown)*?*

prompt for short answers to higher-level thinking skills

- Speech emergence: *What problems did you have while learning* (name process shown)*? How did you solve them?*

prompt for detailed answers to higher-level thinking skills

- Intermediate fluency: *Tell us about learning* (name process shown). *Were there many steps? Which steps were hardest? Was learning* (name process shown) *harder or easier than other things you have learned recently?*

Guided Instruction

Preview and Predict

Tell students that this story is about a boy named Carlos who learns something about skunks and about believing what you hear. Ask them what they think Carlos learns. As you guide students through the illustrations in the story, prompt students to make other predictions: *Where does Carlos live? Why do you think Carlos is watching the skunk? What do you think the skunk will do? Why do you think Carlos is bathing in the river? Why do you think the man is holding his nose? What lesson do you think Carlos will learn?*

GRAPHIC ORGANIZER
Blackline Master 61

Objectives

- To reinforce making judgments and decisions
- To support hands-on learning
- To reinforce working together cooperatively

Materials

One copy of Blackline Master 61 per student; pencils; colored pencils or markers (optional)

Discuss the chart with students, and render it on the chalkboard. Explain that one column of the chart is for recording judgments and the other is for recording decisions. Discuss and redefine judgments and decisions. Page through the story as a group, giving students prompts to help them identify judgments and decisions. For example: *What does Carlos believe he is becoming? So, what does he decide to do? What judgment does Carlos make about Dos Dedos? So, what does he decide to do?* Record their responses on the chalkboard chart. Less fluent students may draw pictures that reflect judgments and decisions made in the story. Encourage these students to use words to explain their pictures.

Reinforce the skill of understanding judgments and decisions by having students review the examples on the chart. Ask students what they would feel or do or say in each situation. Discuss students' reasons.

III. BUILD SKILLS

Comprehension

REVIEW JUDGMENTS AND DECISIONS
Blackline Master 62

Objectives
• To understand judgments and decisions
• To practice following directions
• To practice speaking

Materials
One copy of Blackline Master 62, one spinner, one pair of scissors per group

Have one student in each group cut out the game and distribute the markers. Then explain the directions. Students will place their markers on *Start* and take turns spinning the spinner and moving the correct number of spaces in any one direction. Whenever they land on a space that has writing on it, they must read the words aloud and follow any additional instructions. Remind students to decide carefully before moving their markers. Once students let go of their marker, they cannot move it again, even if they see that moving it the same number of spaces in the other direction would be better for them. Students will move around and around the board several times. The first student in each group to land on the *You Win!* space evenly wins. It is possible for a student to win on the first spin, if he or she spins a "1" and uses good judgment to move in the right direction.

INFORMAL ASSESSMENT

To assess the skill, have students draw a scene from the story in which someone faces a decision. Have them exchange drawings and discuss how the story character responded to the situation.

Comprehension

INTRODUCE DRAW CONCLUSIONS
Blackline Master 63

Objectives
• To draw conclusions
• To identify clues used to draw conclusions
• To practice speaking

Materials

One copy of Blackline Master 63 per student; pencils

Read aloud each question with students. Have students answer "yes" or "no" and mark their sheets independently. Help students find and circle clues in each picture which helped students to draw their conclusions. Then discuss students' answers and the clues that helped them respond.

INFORMAL ASSESSMENT Remind students that Carlos wanted to keep what happened to him a secret. Read aloud pages 396–400. As you read, ask students to look for clues in the story and to draw a conclusion about whether or not Carlos succeeded in keeping his secret.

Vocabulary Strategy

INTRODUCE SUFFIXES
Blackline Master 64

Objectives
• To understand the suffixes -*less* and -*able*
• To practice writing

Materials
One copy of Blackline Master 64 per student; pencils

Read the text at the top of the page with students, and review the meanings of the suffixes -*less* and -*able*. Read the directions aloud with students, and model how to complete one word by adding a suffix. Direct them to the pictures and sentence context for clues. Discuss how students knew which ending to use.

INFORMAL ASSESSMENT Have students reread page 394. Ask them to find the word that ends in either -*less* or -*able*. Ask: *What does it mean? What is the base word?*

Judgments and Decisions

Judgments	Decisions

The Skunk Game

What Do You Think?

1. Draw an X in the "Yes" or "No" box.

1. Would Carlos like to be Gloria's boy friend?
❏ Yes   ❏ No

2. Is Carlos showing off when he tries to catch the skunk?
❏ Yes   ❏ No

3. Were Carlos's feet really too big for his shoes?
❏ Yes   ❏ No

4. Did Papá really mean it when he said that all you need to do to catch a skunk was pick it up by its tail?
❏ Yes   ❏ No

5. Was Carlos happy with his new boots?
❏ Yes   ❏ No

Helpful Endings

1. Read the sentences. **2.** Look at the word endings in the box below. **3.** Write the correct ending on the line.

-less = *without*   **-able** = *capable of being*

1. She ran fast. She was soon

breath_____.

2. They had fun. Their day was

enjoy_____.

3. He spilled some juice. He was

care_____.

4. The shot did not hurt. It was

bear_____.

I. FOCUS ON READING

Focus on Skills

OBJECTIVE: Distinguish between important and unimportant information

TPR
Have students improvise scenes in which they play detectives looking for important information.

Develop Visual Literacy

Take a class poll by asking students if they like books or movies based on mystery. Then ask the class if they can recall the names of any mystery books, movies, or characters. Have students turn to the picture on page 408. Ask the class: *Does anyone recognize this picture?* As students view the photograph, explain verbally or with realia and gesture that it shows a scene from a movie. Ask whether they have seen a movie with a character like this, and identify Sherlock Holmes as a famous fictional detective. Prompt students to describe or point to elements in the photograph, supplying vocabulary as needed—especially *magnifying glass*. If a magnifying glass is available, have them pass it around and look through it. Discuss why magnifying glasses are used. Explain that the actor is playing Sherlock Holmes, and find out what students know about this and other detectives. Ask: *What could he be looking at through the magnifying glass? Suppose he saw a fingerprint or a scratch. Which clue do you think would be important? Why?* Develop the idea that information is important or not, depending on what someone most needs to know.

II. READ THE LITERATURE

VOCABULARY
normally
assignments
automatically
observations
carelessly
swerved

Vocabulary

Print the vocabulary words on the chalkboard, and point to each as you read aloud the pertinent selection sentences. Redirect students to the visual literacy photo on page 408 to further explore word meaning. Read the questions below, using body language and facial expressions to the class. After each question is answered, ask the class what they think the word means. Repeat the sentence with their suggestion or a paraphrase of their suggestion, and then ask the group whether they agree.

Normally: Do you think Sherlock Holmes <u>normally</u> smokes a pipe? Does he look like he smokes a pipe all the time?

Assignments: Do you think Sherlock Holmes considers his <u>assignments</u> to solve mysteries important? Would you like to have <u>assignments</u> like these?

Automatically: What <u>automatically</u> happens when Sherlock Holmes looks through his magnifying glass? Does everything <u>automatically</u> seem bigger?

Observations: What <u>observations</u> do you think Holmes is making? Is he making <u>observations</u> about what he sees through the magnifying glass?

Carelessly: What happens if a detective <u>carelessly</u> loses a clue? Would you expect Sherlock Holmes to act <u>carelessly</u> with clues?

Swerved: Sherlock Holmes never <u>swerved</u> in his plan to solve the mystery. Who can find elements in the picture that show Holmes never <u>swerved</u>?

After students demonstrate understanding of the words, have them create flashcards for each word. Cards should have picture or verbal clues on one side and the word on the other side. Invite students to play a guessing game with the class, holding up the flashcard clues (and offering other clues, such as original sentences, if necessary) until classmates guess the correct word.

CONCEPT
scientific discoveries

Evaluate Prior Knowledge

Discuss a fact that students have recently learned in a science lesson. For example, ask: *What is the bottom of the sea like? How do we know that?* Help students understand that scientists sometimes answer their questions by exploring with their senses or by experimenting. After gathering information with these methods, scientists check to see if their ideas about the information are correct. Ask: *What can scientists do to make sure that their ideas are right?* Brainstorm with students to identify and list some scientific discoveries. Try to include discoveries made by scientists of students' native culture. You might refer to an almanac for ideas. Then have students role-play a scientific exploration of their own. Provide a collection of natural and manufactured objects, such as stones, a comb, and a piece of fragrant food. Create a chalkboard chart for sight, smell, sound, touch, and taste—using pictures and words to label the chart. Have students cycle through the observation area as you question them about their observations.

TPR

nonverbal prompt for active participation

one- or two-word response prompt

prompt for short answers to higher-level thinking skills

prompt for detailed answers to higher-level thinking skills

Develop Oral Language

• Preproduction: *Point to* (indicate various display objects) *something that has a smell* (point to nose picture on chart). *Do you like the smell?* (Model body language for yes or no.) *Point to things that can make sounds* (indicate objects).

• Early production: *Which senses* (point to chart or own face) *would help you explore these objects? Can you tell me one word about how this object* (smells, looks, sounds, and so on)*? Do you know what these objects are? What are they?*

• Speech emergence: *What do you notice about these objects with your senses? What discoveries can you make? Tell us what you observe.*

• Intermediate fluency: *What would you like to learn about these objects? How can you use your senses to gather information you need? What do your senses tell you about the objects?*

Guided Instruction

Preview and Predict

Have students read the title aloud, and explain that the selection tells several short stories that show how to answer questions better. To help students preview the three different elements of each story, you may want to post the following simple outline on the board and have students observe the three elements in the first few pages.

• *Story* that illustrates an important idea (pages 412–414)
• *Questions* that address reader directly (page 415)
• *Analysis* by the author (page 416)

Then have students preview the selection illustrations and format, noting that the three-part pattern repeats throughout the selection. Additionally, discuss what students think might be happening in the illustrations. Ask questions such as: *How old do you think the children on the cover are? What do you think they are doing? What do you think is happening in this picture?*

GRAPHIC ORGANIZER
Blackline Master 65

Objectives

• To distinguish between important and unimportant information
• To reinforce working together cooperatively

Materials

One to three copies of Blackline Master 65 per student; pencils

After reading the selection, discuss the worksheet page. Point out its two columns, and explain the headings. Help students use the illustrations in story number 1 to summarize the snake incident. Then read, or have volunteers read, pages 412–414 aloud. Pause to ask students whether individual pieces of information are important or unimportant. For example, you might point out as important: *Pete is riding his bike. He runs over something that goes whump. It is too dark to see anything.* Some unimportant information is: *Jim swerves to the left. Jim catches up with Pete.*

You may wish to reinforce the skill by handing out additional worksheets and walking students through the process of analyzing the second and third anecdotes.

III. BUILD SKILLS

Comprehension

REVIEW DISTINGUISH BETWEEN IMPORTANT AND UNIMPORTANT INFORMATION
Blackline Master 66

Objectives

• To distinguish between important and unimportant information
• To practice following directions
• To practice speaking aloud

Materials

One copy of Blackline Master 66 per student; scissors; paste or glue

Remind students that in order to tell important from unimportant information, they must think about what someone most needs to know in the particular situation. Explain that important information in one situation might not be important in another. Have students describe what they see in each picture and what they think the characters are saying. Then read the directions, and if necessary, the speech balloons with students. Have them cut out the speech balloon with the most important information and paste it in the box. When all have finished, discuss how they decided which question was more important.

INFORMAL ASSESSMENT

To assess, ask students to identify important and unimportant information on page 416.

Comprehension

REVIEW DRAW CONCLUSIONS
Blackline Master 67

Objectives

• To draw conclusions
• To practice writing

Materials

One copy of Blackline Master 67 per student; pencils; student copy of *How to Think Like a Scientist*

Discuss what students see in the pictures on the page, and then read the directions aloud together. Then explain that they will have to look for clues in the pictures before they can give their answers. Remind them that they can also use what they know to draw conclusions and that they can use more than one clue to draw a conclusion. You may wish to model how to come up with an answer for the first item, encouraging students to tell what they know about baseball games and movies. Have some students work on the page independently, pair others with partners who can take dictation or help them write, and have the rest work together as a group to discuss the clues that can help them draw conclusions.

To assess, display the illustration from page 421, and ask students what conclusions they can draw from it. Discuss how many different conclusions the picture can support.

Vocabulary Strategy

INTRODUCE ROOT WORDS
Blackline Master 68

Objectives
- To practice using root words to decode
- To define the root words *micro, phon, scope, tele,* and *vis*
- To read words with these parts

Materials

One copy of Blackline Master 68 per student; scissors; paste or glue; blank paper

Point out the word parts at the top of the page, and clarify their meanings. If any students speak Romance languages, have them identify words or word parts in their native languages with similar meanings. Emphasize that understanding these word parts can help students figure out the meanings of new words. Read the directions aloud with students. Have students cut out the boxes and pair the definitions with the objects by pasting them side by side on a sheet of paper. If appropriate to students' fluency levels, have them complete the activity in pairs or work as a whole class. Discuss how the root words helped students find the correct answers.

INFORMAL ASSESSMENT Write the word telescope on the chalkboard, and ask students what its word parts suggest about its meaning. Then direct them to find a telescope in the illustrations of *How to Think Like a Scientist.*

Name_____ Date_____

Important and Unimportant Information

Important Information

Unimportant Information

The Right Question at the Right Time

1. Read the questions and look at the pictures. 2. Cut out the most important question.
3. Paste it in the balloon.

Name_____ Date_____

What Makes You Think So?

1. Read the questions and study the pictures. **2.** Write the answer to each question.

Mike's game starts at 2:00. Will Mike go to

the movie before the game? _____

What makes you think so?

_____

_____

_____

_____

Is it summer? _____

What makes you think so?

_____

_____

_____

_____

_____

Maria sits next to Amy. Are Maria and Amy

friends? _____

What makes you think so?

_____

_____

_____

_____

Old Word Parts, New Things

1. Cut out the boxes. **2.** Find the pictures that describe the words. **3.** Paste them next to each other.

micro = small scope = has to do with looking vis = has to do with seeing	phon = has to do with sound tele = from far away

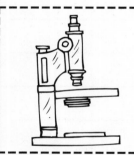 **microscope**

People use this to see and hear people and places from around the world.

People use this to make their voice louder.

telephone

People use this to talk to other people who are far away.

television

 **microphone**

People use this to look at very small things.

AN ISLAND SCRAPBOOK pp. 432A–463P

Written and Illustrated by Virginia Wright-Frierson

BUILD BACKGROUND FOR LANGUAGE SUPPORT

I. FOCUS ON READING

Focus on Skills

Develop Visual Literacy

OBJECTIVE: Distinguish between fact and nonfact

TPR

Ask students what they see in the picture. Encourage them to point out elements such as shells and colors and to name or describe these. Help students see that they are looking at a tabletop created with many pieces of marble fit together. You might use a jigsaw puzzle to clarify this idea. Display pictures or provide examples of marble to show the artist's materials. Ask: *Why does this tabletop look like a real fish tank?* Have students point to parts of the artwork that look most and least real to them. Then discuss how the artist used light and shadow to make the tabletop look real. Ask whether any clues in the picture can help them figure out that they are looking at something that is not real. Invite students to identify these clues and to tell or pantomime how the clues helped.

II. READ THE LITERATURE

Vocabulary

VOCABULARY
naturalist
barrier
parallel
teeming
emerge
fireball

Introduce the vocabulary words by reading aloud the sentences in Teaching Chart 104. Write each vocabulary word on the board, and have volunteers write each a second time. Then help students create skits that incorporate the words and the story context. Use the story illustrations and pertinent sentences to build that context for students. For example, students might line up desks or classmates as a *barrier* to wind blown through the room; scatter themselves like *teeming* crabs; line up unitized objects in *parallel* lines; role-play studying plants or insects for *naturalist*; role-play appearing out of a crowd or closet for emerge; and mime a fiery sun with body language and orange paper or clothing for *fireball*. Then invite students to work in small groups to create captions for each skit—always using the appropriate vocabulary word. You might also ask students to draw a picture of a place they have been where they found shells and crabs and other things similar to those in the picture.

Evaluate Prior Knowledge

CONCEPT
living on an island

Display maps that show islands, preferably ones in your own region or ones that students might know about. Find out whether anyone has ever lived on an island. Define the word island, and let each student point out an island on the map. Use drawings, maps, and mime to clarify what makes a piece of land an island. Explain that islands come in many sizes and land types—some are rocky, while others are sandy, for example. Ask questions such as: *How do people get to islands? What do you think it's like to live on an island?* As students tell, draw, or show their ideas, list on the chalkboard some pros and cons of living on an island.

Develop Oral Language

- Preproduction: *Show us* (point to self and class) *what you would like about living on an island. Show us what you wouldn't like.* (Point to drawing or pantomime as appropriate.)

one- or two-word response
prompt

- Early production: *What is one good thing about living on an island? What is one bad thing? Would you like to live on an island? Tell us one word about why or why not.*

prompt for short answers to
higher-level thinking skills

- Speech emergence: *What are some activities you would do on an island? What would make them different because you are on an island? What might you like least about living on an island?*

prompt for detailed answers to
higher-level thinking skills

- Intermediate fluency: *What do you think life on an island is like? Would you like to live on an island? Have you ever lived on or visited an island? What did you or didn't you like about being on an island?*

Guided Instruction

Preview and Predict

Read the name of the story, and ask students what a scrapbook is. Have them tell what they might put into their own scrapbooks. Explain that this selection is a scrapbook that tells about the writer's real experiences living on an island with her daughter. Use the selection artwork to highlight the scientific nature of the scrapbook. Then have students preview the selection illustrations further. Ask questions such as: *Where do you think this room is? What do the smaller illustrations and photos tell you? Who do you think the woman in the photograph is? What are the names of some things you see in the picture? What are the woman and the young girl doing? How do you think they know each other? Where do you think the woman and the girl are now? What kinds of things do you think this story will tell you?*

GRAPHIC ORGANIZER
Blackline Master 69

Objectives

- To distinguish between fact and nonfact
- To support hands-on learning
- To reinforce working together cooperatively

Materials

One copy of Blackline Master 69 per student; pencils

Complete the activity cooperatively. You may want to copy the scorecard onto the chalkboard. Discuss the page with students, explaining that it shows a fact and nonfact scorecard. The left side is for statements from the story, the right is for students' evaluation of the statement. Review when to check *Fact, Nonfact,* or *Not Sure.* Select five or six statements to read aloud, mixing nonfacts and facts. Write the statement on the chart. You may wish to have students silently mark their scorecards and then share their conclusions. Or you may complete the scorecard entirely as an oral activity.

Reinforce the skill of distinguishing fact from nonfact with student pairs. Have one student make statements about story illustrations as her or his partner tells whether the statements are fact or nonfact.

III. BUILD SKILLS

Comprehension

REVIEW DISTINGUISH BETWEEN FACT AND NONFACT
Blackline Master 70

Objectives
- To distinguish between fact and nonfact
- To practice following directions
- To practice speaking aloud

Materials

One copy of Blackline Master 70 per student; pencils

Review the difference between a fact and an opinion with students. Read the directions aloud with students, and if necessary, the sentences. Then have students mark the box they have chosen. After all students have completed the worksheet, discuss how they reached their conclusions.

INFORMAL ASSESSMENT

To assess, ask students to choose a selection illustration and make a statement of fact and a statement of opinion about it.

Comprehension

REVIEW DISTINGUISH BETWEEN IMPORTANT AND UNIMPORTANT INFORMATION
Blackline Master 71

Objectives
- To distinguish important from unimportant information
- To practice following directions
- To practice speaking

Materials

One copy of Blackline Master 71 per student; one page of blank paper per student; scissors; paste or glue

Remind students of what they have learned about distinguishing important information from unimportant information, stressing that importance often depends on the situation. Encourage students to discuss what they see in the worksheet pictures. Then have them choose and cut out the sentence that is most important to the people in the pictures. Model how to paste the paired sentence and picture together on a sheet of paper. Meet in a group with students who need help to read the sentences. Finally, discuss how all students made their choices.

INFORMAL ASSESSMENT

Have students discuss pages 480–481. Encourage them to create a conversation between Amy and her mother during the hurricane. Ask which information in the conversation was important or unimportant.

Vocabulary Strategy

REVIEW SUFFIXES
Blackline Master 72

Objectives

• To understand suffixes *-less* and *-ment*
• To read words with these suffixes
• To practice writing

Materials

One copy of Blackline Master 72 per student; pencils; student copy of *An Island Scrapbook* (optional)

Help students read aloud the four words at the top of the page. Review the meanings of the suffixes *-less* and *-ment*, and help students identify these word parts. Clarify that they are to complete each sentence with the correct *-less* or *-ment* word from the list at the top of the page. Allow students who need help to work with partners or in a group.

INFORMAL ASSESSMENT

Write the following words on the chalkboard, and define them. Then ask students to use the words to talk about the selection: *endless, enjoyment, harmless, helpless, measurement, spotless, treeless.*

Fact and Nonfact

Statement	Fact	Non-fact	Not Sure

Is That A Fact?

1. Read each sentence. Is it a fact or an opinion? **2.** Place a check in the right box.

1. ❑ Fact   ❑ Opinion

The sunrise is beautiful.

2. ❑ Fact   ❑ Opinion

Fishing boats go out early.

3. ❑ Fact   ❑ Opinion

A crab can grow a new claw.

4. ❑ Fact   ❑ Opinion

Dogs are better pets than cats.

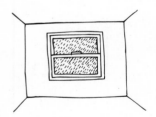

5. ❑ Fact   ❑ Opinion

It has rained all day.

6. ❑ Fact   ❑ Opinion

Everyone loves this book.

You Don't Need to Know Everything

1. Cut out the pictures. **2.** Paste the pictures on a page. **3.** Find the most important sentence about each picture. **4.** Cut it out and paste it under the correct picture.

Morning is the best time to fish.

This beach has very white sand.

A storm is coming.

It rained last Monday, too.

It is very quiet here.

Those are alligator tracks.

The dog's name is Mandy.

Dogs dig up the dunes.

The Ending Is a Clue

1. Read the sentences. Read the words in the box below. **2.** Find the word that belongs in the sentence. **3.** Write the word on the line.

sleepless	soundless	windless	arrangement

1. She put the shells together. She made an _____ of shells.

2. No wind is blowing. It is a _____ day.

3. She cannot sleep. She is _____ .

4. The beach is so quiet in the morning. It is _____ .

THE BIG STORM pp. 464A–491P

Written and Illustrated by Bruce Hiscock

BUILD BACKGROUND FOR LANGUAGE SUPPORT

I. FOCUS ON READING

Focus on Skills

OBJECTIVE: Make judgments and decisions

TPR

Develop Visual Literacy

Bring a globe to the front of the classroom. Explain to the class, using the globe, that Earth spins on its axis. Now show students a picture of a satellite, identify it by name, and use hand gestures to show how it circles the earth. Then ask why satellites might take pictures of Earth from space. Explain that a meteorologist is someone who studies the weather and makes predictions about it using satellite pictures of the earth. Then tell students to turn to the photograph on p. 464. Have students guess what the photograph shows, reading them the title if necessary. Ask students to mime the weather they'd expect these clouds to produce. Then clarify that the picture shows a hurricane, and define the word hurricane (a tropical storm with winds up to 74 mph usually accompanied by rain, thunder and lightning). Ask any student with hurricane experience to share his or her knowledge. Discuss the judgments a meteorologist might make after looking at photographs like this one—for example, which way a storm is traveling or how bad it is. Point out that a meteorologist often provides information to help people make decisions. Ask students again to mime or describe the decisions they would make in the face of a coming hurricane.

II. READ THE LITERATURE

Vocabulary

VOCABULARY
atmosphere
cycle
uneven
data
collision
injured

Print the vocabulary words on the chalkboard, and say each one aloud. As you read the following sentences using body language and facial expressions to give emphasis to vocabulary, ask the group what they think the underlined words mean. Have the class record classmates' suggestions on slips of paper. After you have recorded several suggestions, prompt volunteers to reread the sentences using the new definitions. Write the sentences on the board without the underlined words. Then invite volunteers to bring their slips of paper to the board and complete the sentences using them. Discuss which word seems most likely in each sentence.

Atmosphere: Heat from the sun causes the earth's atmosphere to flow and swirl around it.

Collision: A collision between two moving weather fronts produces violent thunderstorms.

Cycle: People know when to expect storms because every spring the cycle repeats itself.

Data: Data from hundreds of weather stations and satellites went into the computers at the National Meteorological Center.

Injured: Only a few people were killed by the tornado, but many were injured.

Uneven: When warm air rises from the tropics and cold air flows down from the poles, this uneven heating keeps our atmosphere moving.

Once students understand the words, have them improvise a very short weather report. Some can make weather sounds or mime being outdoors. Others can draw pictures showing weather conditions.

Evaluate Prior Knowledge

CONCEPT
storms

Display the visual literacy photo from page 464, and explain that hurricanes are just one kind of storm. Prompt students to describe some weather conditions that occur during a storm. (List these on the board, for example: rain, hail or snow; strong winds; big sea waves.) Then help them list consequences of these conditions, for example: loss of electricity, roads closed, no heat, schools and businesses closed, buildings and cars damaged, flooding, transportation slowed. Encourage students to tell about the worst storm they have seen or experienced. Discuss students' observations and reactions. Ask whether they or others felt unsafe and had to take shelter. Have students draw a picture of the storm and show or tell what happened.

Develop Oral Language

nonverbal prompt for active participation

- Preproduction: *Show us* (point to self and class) *your picture. Show us how the wind blew. Show us what people did during the storm. Show us how you felt.* (Model using body language and facial expression to answer.)

one- or two-word response prompt

- Early production: *What fell from the sky during the storm? Can you tell us one word about the storm? How did you feel seeing it? What did people do to be safe? Show us.*

prompt for short answers to higher-level thinking skills

- Speech emergence: *What kind of weather happened during the storm? How long did it last? What kinds of problems did the storm cause? How did you feel?*

prompt for detailed answers to higher-level thinking skills

- Intermediate fluency: *What happened during this storm? Did it hurt anything? What did people do when the storm started? Were they safe? Have you been in many storms? How do you feel during storms?*

Guided Instruction

Preview and Predict

Encourage a volunteer to read the selection title. Then explain that this selection is a nonfiction article about a huge storm that hit the United States in 1982. Help students understand the graphic on the title page. (It's a cross section of the United States.) Point out where your community would be. Have students preview the selection illustrations and review the concept of storms. Ask questions such as: *What do you think the map shows? What do the pictures in the little boxes tell you? Where do you think we are on this map? What do you think is happening here? How do you think the weather is affecting people and places? Why do you think the wind is strong in this picture?* Call students' attention to the graphics throughout, explaining that these maps and diagrams help explain the larger picture. Finally, ask students to predict what they expect this selection to be about.

GRAPHIC ORGANIZER
Blackline Master 73

Objectives

- To recognize judgments and decisions
- To support hands-on learning
- To practice speaking

Materials

One copy of Blackline Master 73 per student; pencils; student copy of *The Big Storm*

You may use this master either during or after reading to discuss the selection with students, perhaps copying it onto the chalkboard. Then work cooperatively with students to complete the chart. Ask questions about judgments and decisions made by scientists and everyday people during the storm. Help students list these on the chalkboard and paper versions of the chart. Allow less fluent students to draw their ideas or write single words. Discuss each entry.

To reinforce the skill of making judgments or opinions, have students look at the illustration on page 481. Ask what judgments and decisions the families in the houses must make.

III. BUILD SKILLS

Comprehension

REVIEW MAKE JUDGMENTS AND DECISIONS
Blackline Master 74

Objectives
• To make judgments and decisions
• To analyze reasons for decisions
• To practice following directions

Materials
One copy of Blackline Master 74 per student; pencils; drawing paper; colored pencils or markers (optional); student copy of *The Big Storm*

Have a volunteer read steps 1 and 2. Model how to mark the things on the list that are wisest to do. Next, have a volunteer read step 3. Again, model writing or drawing responses. Have more fluent students complete the activity independently while less fluent students work in small groups. Finally, discuss students' reasoning in making these judgments and decisions.

INFORMAL ASSESSMENT

Use page 475 to assess. Ask what judgments and decisions the people in that community will have to make. Discuss what students think the best choices are.

Comprehension

REVIEW DRAW CONCLUSIONS
Blackline Master 75

Objectives
• To draw conclusions
• To practice writing sentences
• To practice following directions

Materials
One copy of Blackline Master 75 per student; pencils; drawing paper and colored pencils or markers (optional)

Review the page and its directions with students. Remind students to look closely at the pictures for clues and to also think about what they know in order to draw conclusions. Students can work independently or in pairs to answer the questions with sentences and phrases or by drawing pictures. If appropriate, complete the activity as a group. When all students have finished the page, invite volunteers to explain their conclusions.

INFORMAL ASSESSMENT

Display page 475. Elicit student conclusions with questions such as: *Who do you think the person in the picture is? What do you think he is doing? What kind of a place do you think he is in? What time of the year do you think it is? Why do you think the artist drew this picture?* Discuss how students reached their conclusions.

Vocabulary Strategy

Objectives

- To use root words for decoding
- To define the roots *atmo, hemi, meter, speed, sphere,* and *therm*
- To practice following directions

Materials

One copy of Blackline Master 76 per student; scissors; paste or glue; blank paper

Read aloud the word parts at the top of the page, and review how to use root words to define unfamiliar words. Have a volunteer read the directions aloud and clarify the steps. Model how to paste the paired boxes side by side on a separate sheet of paper. Discuss how the word parts gave clues to their meanings. If students wish, they may cut apart the boxes and play a memory-matching game with the two halves.

INFORMAL ASSESSMENT

Have students scan the selection to find another unfamiliar word containing the root word *meter* (barometer). Tell them to use the definitions of *meter* and *baro* (weight) to define *barometer*.

Judgments and Decisions

Judgments	Decisions

Storm Coming!

1. A big wind storm is on its way. What should people do? **2.** Place a check before each right thing. **3.** What are other good things to do?

❏ Close the schools.

❏ Sit in the car until it is over.

❏ Go to the movies.

❏ Bring the dog indoors.

❏ Stay in a strong building.

❏ Go shopping for a raincoat.

❏ Put away the outdoor/patio chairs and table.

❏ Find a flashlight or candles.

_____

_____

_____

Can You Figure Out Why?

1. Read the questions. **2.** Look at the pictures. **3.** Write your answers to the questions.

1. Why is the father going back?

_____

_____

2. Why is she taking the candles out?

_____

_____

3. Why are they covering the

window?

_____

_____

4. Why did she buy so much food?

_____

_____

Two Short Word Parts = One Long Word

1. Cut out the boxes below. **2.** Find the sentences that describe each picture. **3.** Paste them next to each other.

speed = has to do with how fast something moves	hemi = half
meter = something that measures	atmo = has to do with air
sphere = something that is round	therm = has to do with heat

It measures how hot something is.

It measures how fast a car goes.

This is a name for half of the globe.

This is the name for the air all around the earth.

CATCHING UP WITH LEWIS AND CLARK pp. 492A–501P

Time For Kids

BUILD BACKGROUND FOR LANGUAGE SUPPORT

I. FOCUS ON READING
Focus on Skills

OBJECTIVE: Distinguish between fact and nonfact

TPR

Develop Visual Literacy

Have students use words and gesture to identify and, if possible, name elements of the picture on page 492. Invite ideas about what the picture represents (spacecraft and space stations). Ask: *Does this place exist in fact?* Then say: *Point to the things in the picture that are like something you know is real. Point to things in the picture that you think will become real some day. Point to things you think will never become real.* Tell students to suppose they can explore this place. Say: *Point to parts you want to know more about.* As each student identifies elements in the picture, poll the class with these directions: *Raise your hand if you think these things are fact. Stand up if you think they are nonfact.*

II. READ THE LITERATURE

Vocabulary

VOCABULARY
diaries
former
journal
bison
superb
glistening

Assemble a collection of realia and illustrations for students to handle: a picture or model of a *bison;* *journal* and *diary* entries or books; an award for a *superb* job; a *glistening* fabric or other object; and a picture of a *former* President or star athlete. As students familiarize themselves with the display, provide flashcards containing the vocabulary words. Read aloud the sentences in Teaching Chart 116 and the pertinent selection sentences to help students to build context. Then ask them to match their flashcards to the correct pieces in the exhibit. When the exhibit is correctly labeled, invite volunteers to lead "tours" for their classmates. Have the tour guides use the vocabulary words in their exhibit explanations.

Evaluate Prior Knowledge

CONCEPT
explore the west

Lead students on an exploration of the classroom or school grounds. Explain that each of them is now an explorer. Help students name some of their discoveries along the way. Link this process to the methods explorers used in earlier times; for example, traveling by foot. Discuss and list reasons why people then and now explore new places and pros and cons in the process. Ask: *Do you think it is hard to go out and explore new places? What might be hard about it? What might be exciting about it? How is it different for today's explorers than for those of the past?* Then ask if they think there are any places left to explore in the world. You may wish to point out that space and the sea are two of these places.

Tell students that Lewis and Clark, whom they will read about in this selection, kept written and visual records of their exploration. Ask student teams to create a journal entry about the school or classroom exploration. Have students contribute pictures and/or words, according to their fluency levels.

TPR

nonverbal prompt for active participation

one- or two-word response prompt

prompt for short answers to higher-level thinking skills

prompt for detailed answers to higher-level thinking skills

Develop Oral Language

• Preproduction: *Show us* (point to self and class) *your picture. What did you find?* (model pointing to picture) *It looks like a* (insert object name).

• Early production: *What did you find? Where did you find it?* (point to classroom or indicate outside) *How did you get to this place? Can you tell us one word about what you found?*

• Speech emergence: *Did you like exploring? Why or why not? What tools did you find most useful in exploring? How did you identify the* (insert object name) *that you found?*

• Intermediate fluency: *What places did you explore? What is the most interesting thing you found? How did you know what it was? What do you think other people could learn from your explorations?*

Guided Instruction

Preview and Predict

Tell students that this article is about Lewis and Clark, the first United States citizens to explore what are now certain parts of the United States. Point out the area of their explorations on the map on page 495. Then focus on the illustration on page 494, and help students draw conclusions from it. (They lived a long time ago, a Native American woman helped them, they rode horses.) Discuss some of the hardships explorers may have faced, such as providing their own food, defending against wild animals, crossing mountains on foot or horseback, and finding their way without maps or trails. Read the title and subtitle on page 495. Explain what it means to be "hot" on someone's trail. Then ask: *Who do you think the people shown here are? What might they have to do with Lewis and Clark? What do you think these objects tell about the time of Lewis and Clark? Have you ever seen anything like these? What do you think this article will tell you?*

GRAPHIC ORGANIZER
Blackline Master 77

Objectives

• To distinguish between fact and nonfact
• To practice following directions
• To practice speaking aloud

Materials

One copy of Blackline Master 77 per student; pencils

Review with students the difference between fact and nonfact, and then have a volunteer read aloud the headings on the blackline master. Complete the activity cooperatively, perhaps posting a copy of the scorecard on the board. Read aloud several statements from the story, including nonfacts as well as facts. Write each statement on the chart, and review the scoring options. Then tell students to mark their own scorecards. As volunteers read each statement aloud, poll the classroom on its scoring. After discussion leads to consensus, complete the chalkboard scorecard as a group activity.

Reinforce the skill of distinguishing *fact* from *nonfact* by having students work together in small groups. Tell them to take turns making statements about the selection illustrations. Other group members can label the statements *facts* or *nonfacts*.

III. BUILD SKILLS

Comprehension

REVIEW DISTINGUISH BETWEEN IMPORTANT AND UNIMPORTANT INFORMATION
Blackline Master 78

Objectives
- To distinguish between important and unimportant information
- To practice following directions
- To practice speaking aloud

Materials
One copy of Blackline Master 78 per student; pencils

Go over the worksheet and its directions with students. Ask students how they distinguish between important and unimportant information. Remind them that the situation is an important factor. Have students describe the illustrations, and as necessary, help them read aloud the written text. After all have finished the worksheet, discuss students' choices.

INFORMAL ASSESSMENT

To assess, display the map on page 495. Ask: *Is the line showing Lewis and Clark's trail important information? Is the label for the state of Texas important? Explain your choices.*

Vocabulary

REVIEW ROOT WORDS
Blackline Master 79

Objectives
- To define the root word *mem*
- To read and understand words in the same word family
- To practice writing

Materials
One copy of Blackline Master 79 per student; pencils

Read aloud the text defining the root word mem, and then help students read the four words and their definitions at the top of the page. Have students identify the root *mem* in each word. Then read the directions aloud, and review their steps. After students complete the activity, have volunteers share their answers.

INFORMAL ASSESSMENT

Reread the last paragraph of main text on page 497. Then ask students to use one of the worksheet words to complete this sentence: *Ken Burns' movie about Lewis and Clark is a living _____ to the explorers.*

Vocabulary Strategy

REVIEW SUFFIXES
Blackline Master 80

Objectives
- To define the suffixes *-less* and *-ment*
- To read words with these suffixes
- To practice writing

Materials
One copy of Blackline Master 80 per student; pencils

Remind students that the word ending *-less* usually means "without" and the word ending *-ment* usually names a thing. Read aloud the directions together. Make sure students understand that they are to write the ending *-ment* or *-less* on the first line and then write the entire word on the second line. Have students share their answers aloud when they are done.

INFORMAL ASSESSMENT

Display the illustration on page 494, and list the following words on the chalkboard: *endless, useless, fearless, hopeless, treeless, countless, sleepless, astonishment, enjoyment, encouragement, amazement, argument.* Ask students to use any of these words to talk about the picture.

Fact and Nonfact

Statement	Fact	Non-fact	Not Sure

Name_____ Date_____

How Much Does It Matter?

1. Read the sentences. Study the pictures. 2. Which sentence is more important?
3. Place a check before that sentence.

❏ There is a waterfall ahead.

❏ They have come five miles today.

❏ Her name means "Bird Woman."

❏ She can speak English and Shoshone.

❏ It is not safe to cross the mountains in winter.

❏ This mountain range is about 3,200 miles long.

❏ Eating this plant will make you sick.

❏ This plant has pretty leaves.

Mem—Is for Memory

1. Read the words in the box. Read about the words. **2.** Then read the sentences below. **3.** Find the word that belongs on the line. **4.** Write the word on the line.

---

remember: to bring something out of your memory

memorize: to store something in your memory

memorial: something that makes us remember a famous person or persons

memo: a note that tells you not to forget something

1. We won't forget Sacajawea. This is a

_____ to her.

2. Is he lost? Does he _____

how to find the trail?

She wants to learn this poem. She will

_____ it.

Mom wants to remember to buy eggs. She writes

herself a _____.

Words with *-ment* and *-less*

1. Read the sentences. Some words do not have an ending. **2.** Write *ment* or *less* at the end of the words. **3.** Write the whole word on the second line.

He pays her with beads. The beads are pay_____ for the meat.

_____

Laws are made here. This is a center of govern_____.

_____

He can't use it. It is use_____.

_____

The ocean seems to have no end. It looks end_____.

_____

He measures the tree. He takes a measure_____.

_____

No sun comes through the trees. This is a sun_____ place.

_____

Retold by Adele Vernon Illustrated by Robert Rayevsky and Vladimir Radunsky

BUILD BACKGROUND FOR LANGUAGE SUPPORT

I. FOCUS ON READING

Focus on Skills

Develop Visual Literacy

OBJECTIVE: Make comparisons and contrasts

Have students go the window. (If possible, take them outside for a nature study.) Direct their attention to the trees and bushes. Ask students how the trees and bushes are alike and different. Explain that telling how things are alike is comparing and telling how things are different is contrasting. Ask students to look carefully at the garden in the picture on page 506. Have them point to a tree or bush in the picture. Ask: *Does this look like a tree or bush near our school? Is it the same or different? Look at the birds in the painting. Do they look like birds you have seen. What type of birds do you think they are? How are they alike and different from birds you see?*

TPR
Use pointing to indicate understanding of similarities and differences

II. READ THE LITERATURE

Vocabulary

VOCABULARY
lamented
inquired
debt
apologized
hasty
refreshment

Print the vocabulary words on the chalkboard, and say them aloud as you write them. Then read the sentences from Teaching Chart 122 emphasizing the vocabulary words and context clues with body language and facial expression. Divide the class into six groups and assign each a vocabulary word. Explain to each group that they are to draw a picture depicting a scene that the vocabulary word could be used to describe. Tape the pictures to the chalkboard. Assign each group another group's picture. Have one person from each group come to the chalkboard and write a vocabulary word from the list that can be used to describe the picture. Now reassign each group to a new picture and have them write a sentence about it.

Evaluate Prior Knowledge

CONCEPT
riddles

Remind students that a riddle is a problem or question that someone needs to solve or answer. Ask students to share any riddles they know. Explain that to solve riddles, sometimes clues are used to gather information. Tell students that they are going to play a game called *What's In the Box?* Provide a box containing a hidden familiar object, such as a book or pencil. Tell students that they may ask questions about the object until they are ready to guess the item. Points may be tallied for correct guesses, or students with correct guesses could choose the next item to be concealed.

Develop Oral Language

nonverbal prompt for active participation

- Preproduction: *Has anyone ever asked you to solve a riddle? Have you ever played a guessing game before?*

one- or two-word response prompt

- Early production: Point to an item in the room. Elicit a one- or two-word answer such as, *What do you do with this? Did you know what it was called when you first came to school this year?*

prompt for short answers to higher-level thinking skills

- Speech emergence: *What would you ask if you didn't know how to use something? What are some good words to use to get more information?*

prompt for detailed answers to higher-level thinking skills

- Intermediate fluency: *Can you think of a riddle? Can you make up a riddle for us to solve?*

Guided Instruction

Preview and Predict

Tell students that in this story, a king offers a reward to a charcoal maker if he can keep the answer to a riddle a secret. Pose the following question, and ask students to share their opinions: *Do you think the charcoal maker will be able to keep the secret? Do you think he will be rewarded?*

Lead students through the illustrations in the story. Encourage discussion by posing questions: *What do you think the king is saying to the charcoal maker? Why do you think he has his hand out? Who do you think these people are? What do you think they are doing? Who do you think made up the riddle? Tell me what you think is happening in this picture. Look at the people bowing. Have you ever bowed to anyone? When would you do this? Where does this story take place? Do you think any of these characters are evil? Show me. Do you think the king likes the charcoal maker? Why or why not?*

GRAPHIC ORGANIZER
Blackline Master 81

Objectives

- To recognize similarities and differences
- To practice following directions

Materials

One copy of Blackline Master 81 per student; pencils

Tell students that they are going to compare the courtier and the charcoal maker. Explain that they will list the ways the characters are alike in the column labeled *Similarities*. Suggest a similarity, such as *both are men*. Instruct students to use short-word responses, such as *men*, to record this detail on the chart. Model differences in a like manner, perhaps using *fancy clothes/work clothes* as an example. Allow students with strong language ability to help those needing support.

Refer students back to an illustration in the text. Ask them to point to something that is similar between one of the characters and themselves. Repeat, asking them to look for a difference.

III. BUILD SKILLS

Comprehension

REVIEW COMPARE AND CONTRAST
Blackline Master 82

Objectives
• To identify similarities and differences between characters in a story
• To practice following directions

Materials
One copy of Blackline Master 82 per student; scissors; paste or glue

Direct students' attention to the pictures in the boxes. Explain that they show different kinds of homes, clothing, and food. Encourage students to think about which items belong to the king and which items belong to the charcoal maker. Read aloud the chart labels. Tell students to cut out the pictures and paste or glue them in the correct area on the chart, thinking about what type of items they are (home, clothing, food) and which character the picture describes.

INFORMAL ASSESSMENT

Have students choose one category: home, food, or clothing. Say: *Show me an example of (home, clothing, food) from the story that describes the king. Find an example that describes the charcoal maker.*

Comprehension

REVIEW MAKE INFERENCES
Blackline Master 83

Objectives
• To practice making inferences
• To use personal experiences to make inferences

Materials
One copy of Blackline Master 83 per student; pencils

Go over the page with students. Explain that when someone is clever, he or she is smart and sharp. Have students think about a time when they were clever. Ask if they have ever thought of something smart or figured something out. Indicate the area on the page where they are to write. Then tell students to explain a time when the charcoal maker was clever. Show them where to write this answer on the page. Encourage students to use the story as reference if necessary.

INFORMAL ASSESSMENT

Direct students' attention back to the story text. Ask them to find an example in the text or an illustration that shows a time when the king was clever.

Vocabulary Strategy

REVIEW CONTEXT CLUES
Blackline Master 84

Objectives
• To practice reading unfamiliar words using clues from the story
• To encourage critical thinking

Materials
One copy of Blackline Master 84 per student; pencils

Read with students the words at the top of the page. Have students point to each word as they read it. Tell them to read the sentences below the words carefully and decide which word from the top of the page belongs in each sentence. Encourage students to use clues about the sentence meaning and then match the given letters and blank spaces with the words they choose.

INFORMAL ASSESSMENT

Direct students back to the story text. Tell them to turn to page 515. Print the word *dowry* on the chalkboard, and say it aloud. Tell students to find the word and use clues from the story to guess its meaning. Select a volunteer to share her or his definition aloud.

Compare and Contrast

Similarities	Differences

Name_____ Date_____

The King or The Charcoal Maker

1. Look at the pictures below. **2.** Think about the differences between the King and the Charcoal Maker. **3.** Cut out each picture and paste each into the correct box in the chart below.

	King	**Charcoal Maker**
Clothing		
Homes		
Food		

Clever Man

1. Write about a time when you were clever. **2.** Think about the story. Find and write an example of when the charcoal man was clever.

1. I was clever when

_____

_____

_____

_____

_____

_____

_____

2. The charcoal man was clever when

_____

_____

_____

_____

_____

_____

_____

_____

Name_____ Date_____

Missing Letters

1. Look at the words at the top of the page. **2.** Read the sentences. Fill in the missing letters to complete the words.

apologized	debt	hasty	inquired	refreshment

1. I have not had a __ __ f __ __ __ h __ __ __ t all day.

2. After making a __ __ __ __ y bow, he called excitedly to his wife.

3. Anna a __ __ __ __ g __ __ __ d to the King for having little food to offer.

4. The king i __ q __ __ __ __ d about how much money the charcoal maker earned.

5. I paid back a d __ __ __ that I owed to my mother.

LIFE IN FLATLAND pp. 532A–533P

Written by A. Square Illustrated by Wallace Keller

BUILD BACKGROUND FOR LANGUAGE SUPPORT

I. FOCUS ON READING

Focus on Skills

Develop Visual Literacy

OBJECTIVE: Author's purpose and point of view

Ask students to hold an object, such as a pencil, directly in front of their eyes. Then have them place the object on the floor. Tell students to stand on their chair and look down at the object. Explain that they have just looked at the object from two different points of view.

TPR
Help students act out the concepts of peace and freedom.

Have students study the painting and name the figures in the picture if possible. Ask if any figures are familiar. Identify the dove for them. Hold your arms out and pretend to float gracefully for them. Then, using a soft voice, say: *I am a peaceful dove.* Ask students what they think the rooster is doing in the painting. Tell students that the animals and the shapes in this painting stand for other things. The artist uses these things to show what he thinks. You may want to point out that Pablo Picasso is trying to make a statement about peace and freedom. Invite students to guess what his point of view is on these issues.

II. READ THE LITERATURE

Vocabulary

VOCABULARY
dimensions
thickness
distinguished
landscape
trifle
unique

Write the vocabulary words on the chalkboard. To introduce vocabulary words, read the sentences on the Teaching Chart as you point to each vocabulary word. Ask a volunteer to use the context clues to act out the sentences as you read them. Check students' understanding by making a drawing on the chalkboard or on a large sheet of paper. As you name a vocabulary word, ask for volunteers to tell or show the definition. Draw a horizon line and a building, such as a house or barn. As you draw the building, use a ruler and say: *The dimensions of the house are 24 inches by 8 inches. That is the height and width.* Add the following and say: *There is a tree next to the house that has a thickness of 3 inches. That is how wide it is. This house is unique because it is the only house that is so tall and narrow. Because it is so tall, the people who live there can see the entire landscape around them* (point to the space in the picture around the house). *They are also careful not to trifle with this special house, but rather they take good care of it because it is distinguished and special.*

Evaluate Prior Knowledge

CONCEPT
math around you

Draw the following shapes on the chalkboard: triangle, square, pentagon, circle. Before the activity, prepare cut-out shapes made of cardboard or construction paper. Hide them in the room. Tell students that they are going to go on a treasure hunt in the room. Explain that there are treasure shapes hidden all around and that they are to find as many as they can. Organize students in teams of three or four. Group students needing extra support with students who have strong language abilities. Limit the search time and set a timer. When the time has expired, ask teams to count their treasure shapes. Allow each team an opportunity to name the treasure shapes they collected. Offer a treasure reward snack such as circular and rectangular crackers or triangular tortilla chips.

Develop Oral Language

nonverbal prompt for active participation

- Preproduction: *Show me* (point to self) *the treasure shape that is closest to the shape of the sun. Do you know the name of that shape?*

one- or two-word response prompt

- Early production: *Which of the shapes on the chalkboard is most like the shape of a roof? Can you name the shape?*

prompt for short answers to higher-level thinking skills

- Speech emergence: *Which shape do you think would be the hardest one to find if it were hidden in the room? Which shape would blend in most with the things around us?*

prompt for detailed answers to higher-level thinking skills

- Intermediate fluency: *How are the shapes similar? How are they different? Can you tell me how the number of sides relates to the name of the figure?*

Guided Instruction

Preview and Predict

Tell students that the author wrote this story to entertain and to get the readers to think about shapes and different points of view. Have students search the illustrations for familiar shapes. Tell students that these shapes, or figures, are the characters in the story. Say: *What shapes are the characters? Why do you think they have different shapes? If you lived in Flatland, what shape do you think you would be? Find the picture of an eye. Why do you think the author put it there? Can you think of different ways to look at these shapes, for example from different points of view? What colors are the shapes? Which shape do you see most often? Do the pictures look flat or like they have dimension or thickness? Why do you think this place is called Flatland?*

GRAPHIC ORGANIZER
Blackline Master 85

Objectives

- To identify author's purpose and point of view
- To make inferences

Materials

One copy of Blackline Master 85 per student; pencils

Read the chart labels with students. Explain that the author has created a world where everything is made up of shapes. Tell them that his reason or purpose for writing this is to explain his imaginative world to us and to entertain us. Have students write *entertain* and *explain* in the top box of the chart. Pair native English speakers with those needing additional language support. Have students read the story, filling out the chart with important details or facts about the author's world. When complete, allow partners to share their charts with the class.

Tell students that point of view also relates to who is telling the story. Have students look through the story and record words that give clues about who is telling the story. When they have a few clues, tell students to write in the top box who is telling the story.

III. BUILD SKILLS

Comprehension

REVIEW AUTHOR'S PURPOSE, POINT OF VIEW
Blackline Master 86

Objectives
- To identify point of view
- To follow directions

Materials
One copy of Blackline Master 86 per student; pencils; colored pencils

Review the directions with students. Demonstrate different views by providing a group example, such as a book. Place a book on a desk or table in front of the class. Model looking down on it, then draw a rectangle on the board and say: *The book looks like a rectangle when I look straight down on it.* Then look from the side at eye level. Use your fingers to demonstrate while saying: *The book looks this wide when I look at it from the side.* Draw a representation on the board. Provide students with a variety of items to observe and draw from different viewpoints. Place them on a desk in front of the classroom. Ask students to take turns coming up to the desk and looking at the items on it from above and from the side. Then have students draw what they saw from above and from the side on the appropriate places on the worksheet. Then ask students to write a few sentences telling about what they see in each picture.

INFORMAL ASSESSMENT

Refer students to the story text. Tell them to think about looking at Farmer Triangle from the side. Give them drawing paper and ask them to draw what they think he would look like from this point of view.

Comprehension

REVIEW MAKE INFERENCES
Blackline Master 87

Objectives
- To make inferences
- To recall details from the story

Materials
One copy of Blackline Master 87 per student; pencils

Name the shapes on the page for students. Point to each shape as you say it aloud and tell students to point and repeat after you. Remind them of the job/shape correspondence in Flatland. Tell them to draw a line (hold up a pencil and draw an imaginary line in the air) to connect the shape with the correct job. Read the jobs slowly and allow students to draw a line to the correct shape. Then encourage students to think about what shape a student in Flatland might be. Have them draw this shape in the box. Use gestures when possible to aid comprehension.

INFORMAL ASSESSMENT

Direct students back to the story text. Tell them to choose a character and find a picture of it. Invite them to imagine what it would be like to be that character in Flatland. Hold a brief discussion encouraging complete sentence responses.

Vocabulary Strategy

INTRODUCE PREFIXES
Blackline Master 88

Objectives
- To recognize and read prefixes
- To increase vocabulary

Materials

One copy of Blackline Master 88 per student; pencils

Read through the page with students. Have them count and tell the number of sides of the first shape. Say: *This is a triangle. It has three sides. Find tri = 3 at the top of the page.* Hold up your copy and point to the top. Then ask students to find the word on the bottom of the page that begins with *tri* and write it next to the shape with three sides. Continue in this manner if necessary, or invite students to work together to complete the page. Explain that *polygon* is a special word because poly means *many.* As a hint, ask students: *Which shape has many sides?* Allow time to check answers as a group.

INFORMAL ASSESSMENT

Direct students' attention back to the story text. Tell them you are going to say the name of one of the jobs people have in Flatland. Tell them that they need to decide which prefix would go with that job. Select volunteers to respond. If the class agrees, have them all respond *yes.* If they believe a wrong response is given, direct them to say *no.*

Author's Purpose; Point of View

CLUES TO AUTHOR'S PURPOSE

1. _____

2. _____

3. _____

4. _____

5. _____

6.

Author's Purpose:

Name_____ Date_____

A New View

1. Look at objects on a desk from above and draw what you see. **2.** Look at objects on a desk from the side and draw what you see. **3.** Write a few sentences telling about each picture.

View from Above	View from Side

A Job Is A Job

1. Look at each shape. **2.** Read each word. **3.** Draw a line between the shape and the name of the job each would have in Flatland.

Doctor

Philosopher

Shopkeeper

Farmer

Soldier

What shape do you think a student would be in Flatland? Draw a student shape in the box.

A Shape Is A Shape

1. Read the prefixes and their meanings below. **2.** Look at the shapes. **3.** Write the words next to their shape from the box below. (*Hint: Watch for the special word.)

pentagon	**triangle**	**octagon**	**hexagon**	***polygon**

penta = 5   **tri = 3**   **octa = 8**   **hexa = 6**   **poly = many**

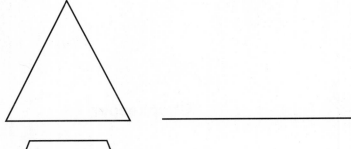

_____

_____

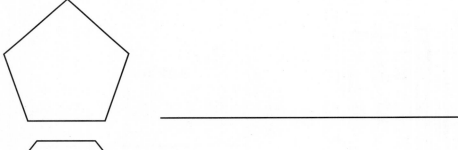

_____

_____

TONWEYA AND THE EAGLES pp. 554A–579P

Retold by Rosebud Yellow Robe Illustrated by Richard Red Owl

BUILD BACKGROUND FOR LANGUAGE SUPPORT

I. FOCUS ON READING

Focus on Skills

Develop Visual Literacy

OBJECTIVE: Review problem and solution

Review with students the idea of problem and solution. Pantomime some problem situations, and invite students to suggest solutions. Some examples might include a flat tire, a torn piece of paper, or a dull pencil.

TPR
Use pointing and pantomime to illustrate understanding of problems and solutions.

Direct students' attention to the illustration. Use pointing and gestures to identify the farmer and sheep going about their business. Explain that this scene may look fine, but that there is a problem. Ask students to point to the person or thing that is in trouble in the picture. Invite them to pantomime what this person might be doing and feeling. Ask questions to elicit ideas about what caused the problem and how it might be solved. Ask: *Why do you think the man is looking up at the sky? Do you know the story of Icarus, the boy who flew too close to the sun? How might the boy's problems be solved?*

II. READ THE LITERATURE

Vocabulary

VOCABULARY
consented
defiantly
cleft
gratitude
sacred
tribute

Write the vocabulary words on the chalkboard. Organize students into six groups. Assign each group a vocabulary word. Tell each group on which page their word is located in the selection and have them skim the page to find the word. Explain that the group is to use context clues, the dictionary, and any prior knowledge they may have to form a definition of the word. Then explain that groups will pantomime, or act out, the definition for the rest of the class. As a group completes its presentation, consult the text and check accuracy. If the meaning is incorrect or unclear, clarify the term so it fits the usage in the story. To check students' comprehension, have groups use each vocabulary word in a phrase or sentence.

Evaluate Prior Knowledge

CONCEPT
problem solving

Explain to students that there are many different types of problems and different ways to go about solving those problems. Tell them that characters in stories often have problems, and that stories sometimes are all about how the characters try to solve them. Further, explain that you are going to give them time to solve different types of problems together in class. Provide students with problem-solving opportunities. Allow students to work in small groups of mixed abilities. Give groups jigsaw puzzles to put together. Challenge the groups to work together to complete the puzzles. Allow students to walk around the room to view other groups' work. An additional activity might include displaying scrambled words on the chalkboard. Tell students that they have a limited time to unscramble the letters to form words. Groups could take turns creating word or number problems for the class to solve.

Develop Oral Language

nonverbal prompt for active participation

- Preproduction: *Show us* (point to class and self) *the pieces of the puzzle problem. Show us how two pieces might fit together.*

one- or two-word response prompt

- Early production: *Have you ever worked a puzzle before? Do you find puzzles easy or difficult to do? Do you enjoy number and word puzzles?*

prompt for short answers to higher-level thinking skills

- Speech emergence: *Tell me how you put a puzzle together. What do you do if the pieces don't fit?*

prompt for detailed answers to higher-level thinking skills

- Intermediate fluency: *Do you enjoy solving problems? Have you ever had to solve a real problem of your own? Was it kind of like putting a puzzle together? Did you try different solutions until one fit? Tell us about it.*

Guided Instruction

Preview and Predict

Tell students that this story is a folktale about a young boy who wanted to be a hero but ran into a problem. Ask students to look carefully at the first illustration with the circle pattern. Tell them to trace with their fingers any circle patterns they see on the page. Ask: *Why do you think there are circle patterns in the middle of this page? What do you think the person on horseback is pointing to? Why is he pointing?* Have students look for other illustrations with circles. Ask: *Why do you think there are circles on this page? What do they mean? What animal shapes do you see on this page? The boy in this story has a problem. What do you think the animals have to do with the boy's problem? Find the illustration of the boy with the rope. Tell me what is happening to the boy. Have you ever hung on to a rope like that before? If so, when and why?* Continue looking through the pictures. Challenge students to guess the boy's problem and how it is solved.

GRAPHIC ORGANIZER
Blackline Master 89

Objectives

- To understand the concepts of problems and solutions
- To practice following directions

Materials

One copy of Blackline Master 89 per student; pencils

Read the chart headings with students. Remind them of a familiar problem, such as not being able to find a book in their desks. Use body language as you act out the situation. Say: *I cannot find my reading book—where can it be? I know . . . it's in here!* Search inside the desk with your hands. Say: *I know how to solve this problem.* Carefully take out things in an organized manner, hold up a book, and say: *I found the book!* Tell them to think about problems and solutions and to write or draw images of problems and their solutions on the chart as they read the story.

Refer students back to the chart. Tell them to identify one of the problems in the story. Invite them to use the chart to show how they would have solved that same problem.

III. BUILD SKILLS

Comprehension

REVIEW PROBLEM AND SOLUTION
Blackline Master 90

Objectives
- To match problems and solutions
- To practice following directions

Materials

One copy of Blackline Master 90 per student; scissors

Read the page with students. Explain that each picture box shows a problem and that the sentence boxes tell solutions to those problems. Instruct students to cut out the cards and match the correct problem with the solution picture. Once they have done that, challenge students to turn over all the cards and play a game of memory with a partner.

INFORMAL ASSESSMENT

Read the following sentence from the story: *The children were not allowed to speak their own language, only English.* Ask students to find the solution to that problem.

Comprehension

REVIEW AUTHOR'S PURPOSE AND POINT OF VIEW
Blackline Master 91

Objectives
- To practice recognizing point of view
- To encourage critical thinking

Materials

One copy of Blackline Master 91 per student; pencils; colored pencils or crayons

Tell students that *Tonweya and the Eagles* is a story that was told to keep the traditions of a family alive. Explain to students that on this page they will write their own story. Guide them through the story outline, and show them where they will insert facts about themselves and their families. Encourage students to discuss their stories at home with their families to learn or clarify information. Indicate where students should include an illustration. Students can share family stories with each other.

INFORMAL ASSESSMENT

Read the following sentence from the story: *After they were dead, I found several of the stories written out in my mother's and father's handwriting.* Ask a volunteer to respond to the following question: *From whose point of view would these stories be told?*

Vocabulary Strategy

REVIEW CONTEXT CLUES
Blackline Master 92

Objectives
• To develop word meaning
• To build problem-solving skills

Materials
One copy of Blackline Master 92 per student; scissors; glue or paste; construction paper

Direct students to cut out the puzzle pieces. Explain that the puzzle pieces will fit together so that the definitions are correct and complete. Pair students with strong English language ability with those needing extra language support. Ask students to read the sentences they formed and then write them on a separate sheet of paper. Allow students to put together the puzzle pieces and read the sentences several times until they are familiar with the new words.

INFORMAL ASSESSMENT

Refer students back to the text. Invite a volunteer to respond to the following question: *What do we call a Medicine Man in modern-day language?*

Problem and Solution

Problem	Solution

Problem-Solution Game

1. Cut out each box. **2.** Play a memory game to match Solutions with Problems.

Tonweya wants the eaglets.	
Tonweya searched for his family.	
The eaglets were hungry.	
Tonweya was stuck on the cliff.	

My Story

1. Fill in the blanks to tell your story. **2.** Draw a picture of your family in the frame.

My name is _____. I am

_____ years old. My old

home was _____. We

traveled here by _____.

The thing I remember most is _____.

One great thing about my family is _____.

My Family

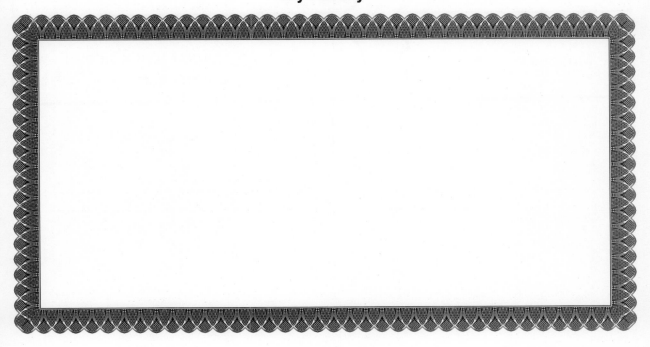

Vocabulary Puzzler

1. Cut out each puzzle piece. **2.** Put together the puzzle pieces. **3.** Read the new sentences.

A tipi is	**something given respect.**
Sacred means	**the leader of a tribe.**
A cleft is	**soft shoes made of animal skin.**
A chief is	**an opening or ledge in a cliff.**
Moccasins are	**a cone-shaped tent made of animal skin.**

BREAKER'S BRIDGE pp. 580A–601P

Written by Laurence Yep Illustrated by David Wisniewski

BUILD BACKGROUND FOR LANGUAGE SUPPORT

I. FOCUS ON READING
Focus on Skills

OBJECTIVE: Compare and contrast

TPR
Have students show "thumbs up" and "thumbs down" to demonstrate understanding of similarities and differences.

Develop Visual Literacy

Ask students to name what they see in the photo. Point out that these houses were built beneath rocks and cliffs. Ask them to think about the houses and apartments they live in. Then tell them that you are going to make some statements about the picture and that they must listen carefully as you say things about the picture. Explain to them that they are to say *Yes* if they agree with what you say and *No* if they disagree with what you say. Say things such as: *The houses in the picture have windows, and my house has windows, too. I see doors like the front door of my house. The yard by the house in the picture is like the yard where I live. People live close together in the houses like people live close together in apartment buildings.* Tell them that you are comparing the apartments of today to the apartments built by the Anasazi. Ask them to name other similarities and differences. Encourage students to share their responses and notice the similarities and differences among classmates.

II. READ THE LITERATURE

VOCABULARY
scheme
piers
gorge
dismay
murky
immortals

Vocabulary

Print the vocabulary words on the chalkboard. Sketch the outline of a bridge spanning a *gorge* next to the words. Using the definitions, label the *piers* and include a *gorge*. Use the vocabulary words and point to the bridge sketch as you say something like the following: *This is a scheme, or plan, for building a bridge.* Identify each vocabulary word as you use it by pointing to it. *The piers hold up the bridge and allow it to stretch over the gorge, which is a deep, rocky valley.* Explain that you are going to pretend that you are afraid to cross the bridge. *I need to cross the bridge quickly to save my family on the other side. I am afraid because it is murky, so it is difficult to see. I hope I don't become dismayed and lose my courage to cross. If I cross and save my family, I will become an immortal hero. That means I will live forever.* Invite students to act out and narrate similar scenes in small groups. Ask volunteers to come to the class and act out the sentences as you just have. If necessary repeat it with them once before they do it on their own. Elicit other students to create new sentences with the vocabulary words.

Evaluate Prior Knowledge

CONCEPT
bridges

Using encyclopedias and other non-fiction books and periodicals as sources, provide students with pictures of bridges. Explain to them the function the bridges serve. Say: *Bridges are used to connect things, such as pieces of land. Some bridges are built over water to connect two pieces of land, so people can cross over the water. Some bridges are built over busy streets or train tracks to help people cross safely.* Ask volunteers to share any experiences they may have had with bridges. Engage students in a hands-on bridge-building experience. Create groups consisting both of students with strong language ability and those requiring extra language support. Give each group a pile of craft sticks, tag board, scissors, and glue. Challenge groups to use these materials, as well as the illustration models, to construct their own bridges. Allow time for groups to present their bridges to the rest of the class. Encourage them to consider what function their bridge serves: provide passage over water, road, railroad tracks, and so forth.

Develop Oral Language

nonverbal prompt for active participation

- Preproduction: *Show me* (point to self) *the two support sides of the bridge. Show me where people cross your bridge* (direct student to either the group's model or illustration).

one- or two-word response prompt

- Early production: *Have you ever crossed a bridge? What was underneath the bridge, land or water?*

prompt for short answers to higher-level thinking skills

- Speech emergence: *Do you know the names of any famous bridges and where they are located? What is under these bridges? Do you think building a bridge would be easy or difficult?*

prompt for detailed answers to higher-level thinking skills

- Intermediate fluency: *Tell me what most bridges are made of. What would likely cross the bridge you built—cars, animals, or people on foot? Why?*

Guided Instruction

Preview and Predict

Tell students that this story is about a man named Breaker. Explain that this is his nickname because he always breaks things. Demonstrate by dropping something breakable, such as a cookie. Tell them that an emperor (like a king) wants Breaker to build a bridge across a very deep and powerful river. Lead students through the illustration in the selection, asking questions based on the illustrations: *What do you think Breaker is doing in this picture? Why do you think he is holding up his arms? What might he be doing with the big knife? Who do you think Breaker is speaking with? What do you think they are saying? What do you think is happening here? Do you think it is something good or bad? Do you think Breaker will be able to build the bridge?*

GRAPHIC ORGANIZER
Blackline Master 93

Objectives

- To compare and contrast characters
- To encourage working cooperatively

Materials

One copy of Blackline Master 93 per student; pencils; colored pencils

Tell students that they will use this diagram to compare (find similarities) and contrast (find differences) between two characters from the story. Have them search the illustrations for a picture of Breaker and the Emperor. Encourage students to use the illustrations and text to think of words that can be used to describe each character. Explain that the shared area in the middle of the diagram is where they record things about the characters that are the same. The outside parts are for recording things about the characters that are different. Allow students to use short answers, and even illustrations, if necessary.

Invite students to share their completed Venn diagrams. Ask them to listen for adjectives that might have similar meanings. Ask: *If you could choose one of these two characters as a friend, which one would you choose, and why?* Hold a brief discussion, encouraging support from the text.

Students might use the Venn diagram to compare this story with another story they have read.

III. BUILD SKILLS

Comprehension

REVIEW COMPARE AND CONTRAST
Blackline Master 94

Objectives
- To practice finding similarities and differences
- To encourage critical thinking

Materials

One copy of Blackline Master 94 per student; pencils

Read through the page with students. Explain the Venn diagram. Say: *Look at the two circles. The part of the circle on the left will tell things that are true about a river.* Point to this area on the page. Say: *This part of the circle on the right will tell things that are true about people.* Again, indicate by pointing. Say: *The area in the middle that both circles share will tell about things that are true of both rivers and people.* Tell students to use the words at the top of the page to complete the diagram.

INFORMAL ASSESSMENT

Refer students to the illustration of Breaker and the old man. Ask a volunteer to point or offer a short one or two-word response to the following: *Show me something that is the same and different about the two people on this page.*

Comprehension

REVIEW MAKE INFERENCES
Blackline Master 95

Objectives
- To practice making inferences
- To work together cooperatively
- To practice following directions

Materials

One copy of Blackline Master 95 per student; pencils; colored pencils or crayons

Direct students' attention to the pictures in the boxes. Read the captions underneath the boxes. Have students draw a picture of what will happen next in the empty box next to each picture box. Encourage students to include a short written response underneath their drawings of what actually happens in the story.

INFORMAL ASSESSMENT

Read the following sentence from the story: It was getting so dim that Breaker could not be sure if the old man smiled. Allow students to read the sentences around this one. Then ask: *Do you think the old man smiled or not? Why?*

Vocabulary Strategy

REVIEW PREFIXES
Blackline Master 96

Objectives
• To develop an understanding of prefixes
• To practice listening critically

Materials
One copy of Blackline Master 96 per student; pencils

Read through the page with students. Explain that a prefix is placed at the beginning of a word and helps to change its meaning. Print *re-* and *in-* on the chalkboard. Point to *re-* and say: *This means to do something again, as in the word remake—to make the bed again.* Point to *in-* and explain that it means "into." Tell students to listen carefully for the prefix as you read the first sentence. Read it the first time, omitting the prefix. Read it a second time with the correct prefix, and challenge students to decide which prefix on the board matches what you said aloud. Have them write the correct prefix in the blank. Repeat this procedure for sentences 2 through 5. Invite students to guess which prefix belongs in the blank before you read each sentence the second time.

INFORMAL ASSESSMENT

Tell students that the word *called* appears in the story. Print the word on the chalkboard. Ask students to decide which prefix would make the word mean "call again." Select a volunteer to write the correct word on the chalkboard.

Compare and Contrast

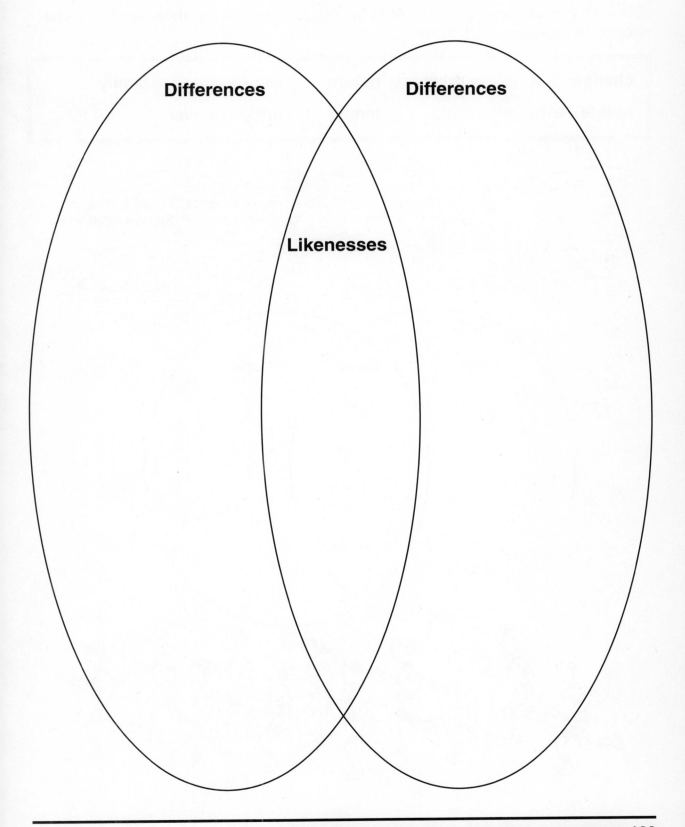

Differences

Differences

Likenesses

Rivers are Like People

1. Read the words listed below. 2. Write the words in the chart to show how rivers and people are the same and different.

change	grow	nature	wet	family
bridge destroyer	wild	tame	bridge builder	

River   Same   People

I Predict

Breaker meets the old man.

Draw what you think will happen next.

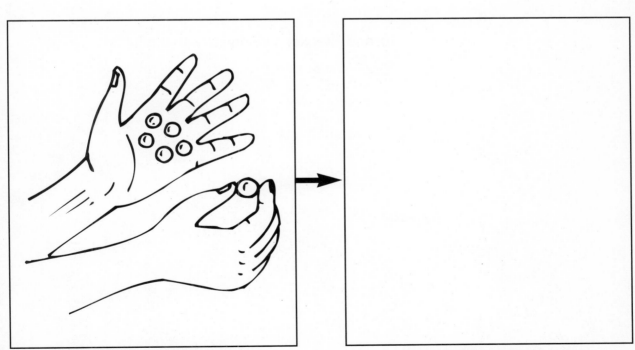

The magician makes pellets.

Draw what you think will happen next.

Re- and In-

1. Read the sentences below. **2.** Write the correct prefix in each blank.

re	in

1. Breaker needed to__ __ **pair** the bridge.

2. The emperor sent an official to __ __ **spect** the bridge.

3. Breaker decided to __ __ **clude** larger stones in the pier.

4. Breaker __ __ **built** the bridge each time it fell.

5. The old man __ __ **turned** Breaker's kindness with a gift.

Time For Kids

BUILD BACKGROUND FOR LANGUAGE SUPPORT

I. FOCUS ON READING

Focus on Skills

Develop Visual Literacy

OBJECTIVE: Identify problem and solution

TPR

Tell students to study the mural. Explain that children made this with the purpose of showing some of Earth's problems and possible solutions for these problems. Invite volunteers to read the different statements on the mural. Help students with meaning as necessary. For example, introduce the problem of littering by crumbling a piece of paper and throwing it on the ground. Say: *This is called littering. It is a problem.* Pick up the paper and put it in the class recycle bin and say: *A solution to that problem is to clean up the litter and recycle our garbage.* Have students look carefully at the mural. Tell students that you are going to identify something in the picture. Explain that they are to say problem or solution, depending on what is being shown. Then encourage students to think of their own Earth problems and solutions to add to the mural.

II. READ THE LITERATURE

Vocabulary

VOCABULARY
fumes
regulations
stricter
width
protective
standards

Print the vocabulary words on the chalkboard. Discuss one word at a time. Direct students to the first paragraph of the article. Tell them to search for the word *fumes*. Explain that the car lets off *fumes*. Fan your face and make a sour looking face and say: *Car fumes smell really bad and are bad for us to breathe.* Select a volunteer to read the sentence from the text containing the word fumes, and check for comparable meaning. Repeat in this manner for the remaining vocabulary words. Use body language when possible to clarify meaning. Suggested examples are: *No running or gum chewing are regulations, or rules, in the classroom. At the end of the year, I will be stricter about your handwriting. If it is messy, you will do it again. The width of the door is (measure for students with a ruler). I am very protective of all of you. I will not let anyone harm you (go to a student and shelter her or him with your arms). There are standards I use to grade you. Every paper is graded in the same way. If you get everything correct, it is 100%.* After each example, refer students to the text to check context.

Evaluate Prior Knowledge

CONCEPT
air pollution

Find a city street scene in picture form in a magazine or book, or as a photo on a film-strip or slide. Walk around the classroom, allowing each student to look at it. Display the picture or photo as you point to things that create air pollution. Point to cars, buses, trains, factories or buildings emitting fumes, and any cigarette smoke, if visible. Ask students what kinds of problems air pollution creates. They might act out or provide short-word responses. If no one mentions it, point out that air pollution can harm not only people, but every living thing on Earth. Provide students with drawing materials, and ask them to create a city with no pollution. Challenge them to draw this scene and label the parts of their pollution-free city scene.

Develop Oral Language

nonverbal prompt for active participation

- Preproduction: *Show me* (point to self) *how it feels to breathe air pollution. Air pollution smells bad to me.* (make an unpleasant face)

one- or two-word response prompt

- Early production: *Have you been in a crowded place where there was a lot of air pollution? Have you ever seen the smoke from the back of a car or truck? Do you know what it is called?*

prompt for short answers to higher-level thinking skills

- Speech emergence: *Why is air pollution bad? How would the air look without air pollution?*

prompt for detailed answers to higher-level thinking skills

- Intermediate fluency: *What do you think makes the most air pollution? Do you know how to solve the problem of air pollution?*

Guided Instruction

Preview and Predict

Tell students that this article focuses on a real problem that we are facing worldwide. Explain that the illustrations show true things that are happening every day. Direct students' attention to the photo of the bridge traffic. Say: *Air pollution smells very bad* (make an unpleasant face) *and can actually hurt us if we breathe it* (put your hand on your chest and breathe with difficulty). *Look at the photo and point to some of the things that you think make the air polluted. Look at the photo of the bike route. Do you see any cars? How does this person get around? Why do you think this photo is in the article? Look at the graph about dangers in the air. What do you think it shows? Why might this graph be included in the article?*

GRAPHIC ORGANIZER
Blackline Master 97

Objectives

- To identify problems and their solutions
- To practice making inferences
- To work cooperatively

Materials

One copy of Blackline Master 97 per student; pencils

Read the chart labels with students. Point to the large box at the top, and say: *The problem* (identify label in the box) *is air pollution.* Print it on the chalkboard, and have students copy it in the box. Explain that in the boxes on the left side they will draw or write things that people are doing to try to correct the problem. In the boxes on the right, they are to show or tell what happened—if it worked or not. At the bottom, they should think of a way that would work to solve the problem of air pollution. Allow students to work together as they read the selection.

III. BUILD SKILLS

Comprehension

REVIEW AUTHOR'S PURPOSE AND POINT OF VIEW
Blackline Master 98

Objectives
- To recognize author's purpose and point of view
- To practice following directions

Materials

One copy of Blackline Master 98 per student; pencils; scissors; glue or paste

Explain to students that the purpose of this article is to educate people about the dangers of smog and the importance of clean air. Such an article is written to give information. Tell students that when reporters develop a news story they try to answer the questions *Who? What? When? Where? Why?* and *How?* as a framework for researching their ideas. Have students look over the reporter's notebook on the blackline master. Read over the questions with students. Then read through the fact notes at the bottom of the page. Instruct students to cut out each fact box. Point to the drawing of the notebook, and say that the facts are the answers to questions. Read the first question, and ask students to work together to decide which response at the bottom matches. Model checking each response to see if it answers the question correctly. Suggest that students look for clues and consider what type of response is needed for each question (who, what, where, why, when). Encourage students to first place the fact boxes next to the questions they think are appropriate. Once they have checked and are sure of the responses, students can paste the fact boxes on the page.

INFORMAL ASSESSMENT

Direct students back to the text. Tell them to look at the photo of the biker. Ask them how they think the author feels about air pollution and what the author is trying to say by showing a person riding a bike.

Comprehension

REVIEW CONTEXT CLUES
Blackline Master 99

Objectives
- To review use of context clues to understand unfamiliar words
- To increase vocabulary
- To work cooperatively

Materials

One copy of Blackline Master 99 per student; scissors; paste or glue

Explain to students that each vocabulary word at the bottom of the page matches a definition at the top of the page. Read through the words and definitions with students. Ask students to cut out the puzzle pieces and place them over the correct definition. You may want to model an example for children. Cut out the word fumes, hold it up to show the class, and say it out loud. Ask students: *Which definition above matches the word fumes?* Then say: *Fumes are smoke or gases* as you place the puzzle piece over its definition. Explain that the vocabulary word and its definition will be the same shape. Students can work in pairs to match the remaining words and definitions. Suggest that they practice reading the words and the definitions.

INFORMAL ASSESSMENT

Tell students to cover the definitions with the vocabulary puzzle pieces. Refer them back to the photo of the bridge traffic. Ask students to answer the following question by stating the correct vocabulary word: *What is one of the causes of air pollution that is being given off by the cars, trucks, and vans in the photo?*

Vocabulary Strategy

REVIEW PREFIXES
Blackline Master 100

Objectives
• To review prefixes *re-* and *in-*
• To practice following directions

Materials
One copy of Blackline Master 100 per student; pencils

Remind students that the prefix *re-* means again and the prefix *in-* means in. Then review the words in the word bank. Tell students that each of these words will fit into the boxes in the puzzle (point to puzzle). Read the words in the word bank with students. Then read the first clue in the *Across* section. Pause, and read the correct word from the word bank. Have students complete the puzzle with words from the word bank. Tell students to count the number of letters and the number of boxes available to check the accuracy of their choice. Model writing one letter per box. Repeat with the remaining clues.

INFORMAL ASSESSMENT

Tell students that the word *issue* appears in the article. Print *issue* on the chalkboard. Say: *Issue means "to give." Which prefix can be added to make this word mean "to give again"?*

Problem and Solution

Problem	Solution

Fact Jumble

1. Read the questions in the reporter's notebook. **2.** Read the reporter' notes below.
3. Cut out the notes. **4.** Paste the notes next to the correct questions.

1. What is smog? _____
_____

2. Where is smog found? ____
_____

3. Who helps fight this problem
_____

4. Why is the EPA trying to
clean the air? _____

5. How is the EPA trying to
make things better? _____
_____

6. When will these laws
take place? _____
_____

---

to keep the air safe for all living creatures

fog-like air pollution

passing new laws

laws will take effect in 2004

Environmental Protection Agency (EPA)

it travels in the air and effects all parts of the world

Puzzling Vocabulary

1. Cut out the word puzzle pieces at the bottom of the page. **2.** Find the correct definition for each word. **3.** Place the word puzzle piece on its correct definition.

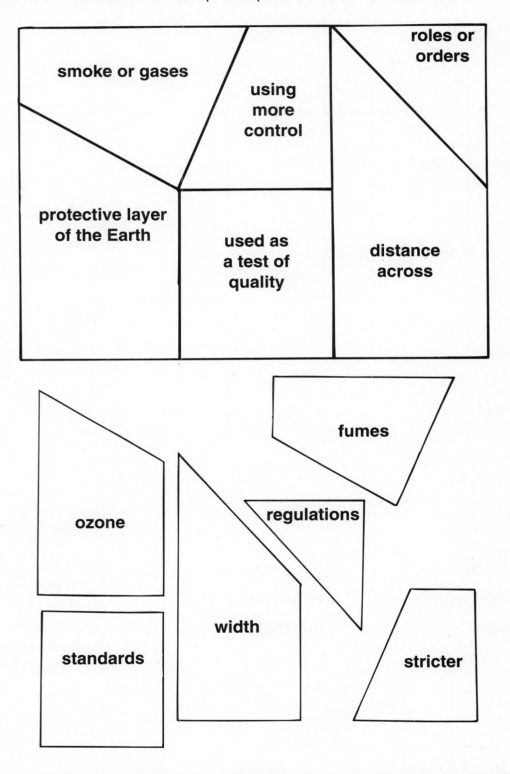

Prefix Crossword

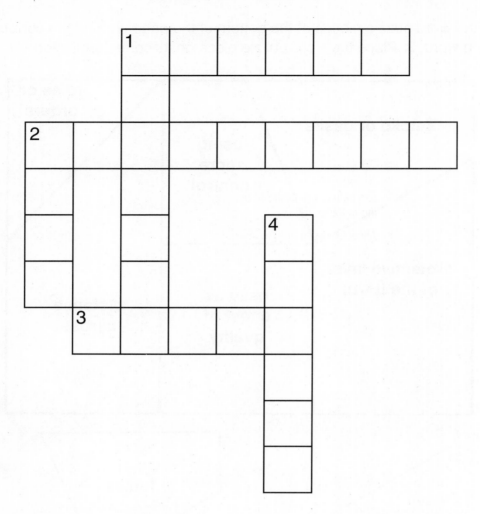

Across

1. to put a disease in

2. to notice again

3. to act again

Down

1. to add in

2. to do again

4. to tell again

Word Bank

retell
redo
infect
recognize
include
react

AMISTAD RISING: A STORY OF FREEDOM pp. 616A–647P

Written by Veronica Chambers Illustrated by Paul Lee

BUILD BACKGROUND FOR LANGUAGE SUPPORT

I. FOCUS ON READING

Focus on Skills

OBJECTIVE: Review judgments and decisions

TPR

Develop Visual Literacy

Use physical examples to introduce the ideas of balance and harmony. If a scale is available, show how two objects of equal measure balance on the scale. Use a musical instrument or a CD/cassette to show notes or voices that demonstrate harmony. Ask students if the notes/voices sound good together. Explain that balance and harmony can be used to describe people. People working together are balanced. They are working in harmony.

Allow students time to study the painting. Use your hand and trace some of the lines on the page as you say: *Trace the lines in the painting. Are they repeated? Does each line seem to belong in the painting? What colors do you see? Do you see colors used again and again? Do they seem to belong together? Stand and show me* (use arm gestures) *how you would stand next to a good friend. Do the people in the picture seem to be with friends? Do you think they get along well? Do you think they get along well with nature, too? What feeling do you think the artist had in mind?*

II. READ THE LITERATURE

VOCABULARY
nightfall
navigate
escorted
coax
perished
ushered

Vocabulary

Print the vocabulary words on the chalkboard. Briefly provide a definition for each, using physical activity when possible. As you act out each vocabulary word make statements explaining what you or the person in the picture is doing.

nightfall: Show a picture taken at night. Pretend you are the sun going down and turning off the lights for nightfall. Say: *Now it is nightfall.*

navigate: Show a picture of someone steering a boat. As the class circulates the picture steer an imaginary boat and say: *The man (or woman) is navigating a boat.*

escorted: Walk a student to the door. When you reach the door say: *I escorted this student to the door.*

coax: Urge a student out of her or his seat to go the chalkboard. Say while doing this: *I am trying to coax this student to the chalkboard.*

perished: Show a picture of a building on fire or forest fire. Faint and lie still to imitate someone perishing. Say: *Many people perish in fires.*

ushered: Walk a student to her or his seat. Then say: *I ushered (name student) to her (or his) seat.*

Prepare index cards with the vocabulary words on them. Place students into six cooperative groups. Allow each group to select a card. Invite the group to pantomime the vocabulary word. Select other groups to guess the word. Discuss the definitions with the whole class.

Evaluate Prior Knowledge

CONCEPT
returning home

Tell students to think about their homes. Write the word home on the chalkboard. Ask students to raise their hands if they wish they were at home now, or ask students individually to reply yes or no. Say: *How do you feel at your home? When you're away from home for a while, how does it feel to return?* Explain that sometimes when you are away from home, you want to return to feel safe and happy. Organize the class into two teams, and play a game of kickball (if going outside is possible) or duck-duck-goose (if going outside is not an option). Play one of the two games long enough to give each student an opportunity to leave "home" (home plate or the space in which she or he was sitting). After the game is played, discuss how it felt to be in danger (chased) and how it felt to return home.

Develop Oral Language

nonverbal prompt for active participation

• Preproduction: *Show or tell me* (point to self) *what you like doing best at your home. Show me how you feel when you're at home.*

one- or two-word response prompt

• Early production: *Have you ever gone away from your home for a while? Did you go to camp or visit a friend or relative? How long were you away?*

prompt for short answers to higher-level thinking skills

• Speech emergence: *How do you think you would feel if you were away from your home for a long time? What do you think you would miss the most?*

prompt for detailed answers to higher-level thinking skills

• Intermediate fluency: *What do you like best about being at home? Can you describe a situation in which you might be away from home for a while? How would you feel?*

Guided Instruction

Preview and Predict

Have students scan through the illustrations in the text. Ask questions to prompt ideas about the story: *Where does this story take place? Why do you think the ocean might be important in this story? Whom do you see on this ship? Does this look like a modern ship? When do you think the story takes place? Where do you think the ship is going? The name of this ship is Amistad. In Spanish, Amistad means "friendship." Do you think all the people on this ship look friendly? What do you think is happening?*

GRAPHIC ORGANIZER
Blackline Master 101

Objectives

• To recognize judgments and decisions
• To work cooperatively

Materials

One copy of Blackline Master 101 per student; pencils; colored pencils

Tell students that a decision is a choice that you make in a particular situation. Give a concrete example, such as finding lost money. Pick up a dollar from the floor and say: *I have a decision to make. Should I keep the dollar or try to find the person who dropped it?* Explain that to complete the chart, students are to find things that happen in the story that require a decision to be made. They record these events in the left-hand column. To the right of each event, they record the decision that is made. Pair students of limited language development with more fluent speakers. Allow them to use illustration and short-word responses. Invite students to share their work.

III. BUILD SKILLS

Comprehension

REVIEW JUDGMENTS AND DECISIONS
Blackline Master 102

Objectives
• To recognize judgments and decisions
• To practice following directions

Materials
One copy of Blackline Master 102 per student; pencils

Read through the page with students. Remind students of the names of each character on the left side. As you read each name, tell them to touch the corresponding picture. Ask students to listen carefully as you read the decision on the right and then to find the person (or people) who made this decision. Model drawing a line to connect the decision with the person. Continue with the remaining decisions.

INFORMAL ASSESSMENT

Read the following sentences from the story: *He decided to strike that night. With a loose nail he had found earlier in a deck board, he picked the lock on his shackles, freeing himself and then the other prisoners.* Ask students to show or tell who made this decision and what it meant.

Comprehension

REVIEW DRAW CONCLUSIONS
Blackline Master 103

Objectives
• To practice drawing conclusions based on story information
• To work cooperatively

Materials
One copy of Blackline Master 103 per student; pencils; colored pencils

Tell students to think about the character Joseph Cinqué. Brainstorm a list of adjectives to describe his personality. Use physical gestures and pantomime when possible to clarify terms suggested. Pair students needing language support with more fluent speakers. Instruct students to complete the character web by drawing picture representations and using the adjectives from the chalkboard. Invite students to share their webs with each other.

INFORMAL ASSESSMENT

Read the following sentence from the story: *Cinqué demanded to know what would happen to them.* Ask students what character trait this illustrates.

Vocabulary Strategy

REVIEW CONTEXT CLUES
Blackline Master 104

Objectives
• To reinforce use of context to identify word meaning
• To practice following directions

Materials
One copy of Blackline Master 104 per student; pencils

Go through the page with students. Read the vocabulary words at the top of the page and discuss their meanings. Direct students' attention to the first drawing. Read the sentence next to it, pausing at the blank. Encourage students to use the picture clues to decide which vocabulary word completes this sentence. Model for the students how to write it in the missing space. Have students complete the page, crossing off each word as
it is used.

INFORMAL ASSESSMENT

Ask two volunteers to pretend they are two ships and illustrate the meaning of ...*the Amistad was <u>escorted</u> by an American ship into the harbor of New London, Connecticut....*

Judgments and Decisions

Decision Chart

What Happened	Decision

Difficult Decisions

1. Draw a line from each person or people to the decision they made.

Decided to fight for his freedom.

Decided to defend the African prisoners.

Decided to free the Africans.

What Was Joseph Like?

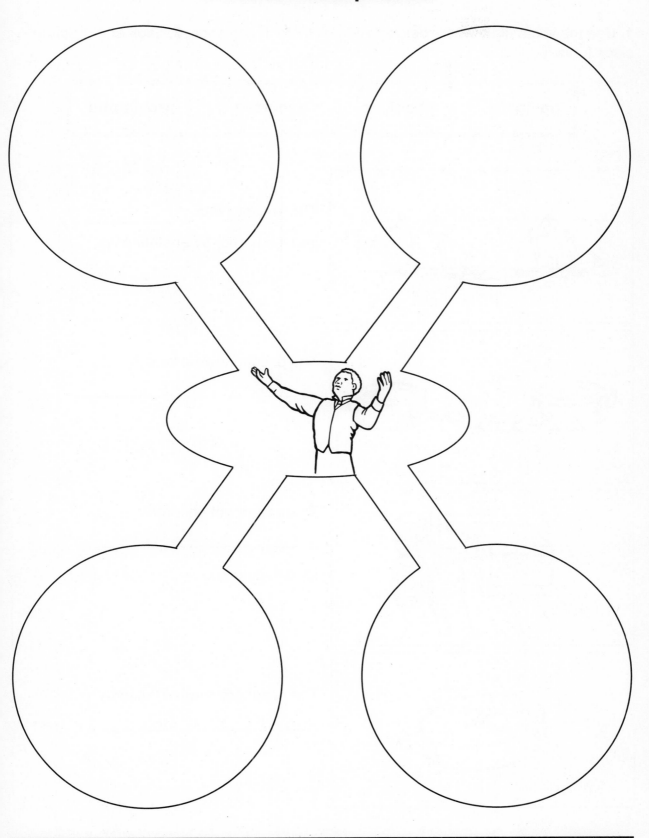

Name_____ Date_____

Clues to Colonial Vocabulary

1. Use the vocabulary words below to complete each sentence. **2.** Look at the picture clues for help.

navigate	shackles	escorted	provisions

The Amistad was _____

into the harbor by another ship.

The prisoners were kept in

_____.

There were not enough

_____

for the journey.

The prisoners needed the crew to

_____.

RIP VAN WINKLE pp. 648A–673P

Written by Washington Irving Dramatized by Adele Thane Illustrated by Gary Kelley

BUILD BACKGROUND FOR LANGUAGE SUPPORT

I. FOCUS ON READING

Focus on Skills

OBJECTIVE: Review cause and effect

TPR

Develop Visual Literacy

Ask students to turn to the picture by Thomas Davies on page 648. Use a soft, soothing voice as you tell students to look at the picture. Select volunteers to identify items in the picture by pointing to various things, such as the boats, trees, shoreline, and sky. Ask students how they feel looking at the scene; *relaxed and peaceful?* Then change voice to a loud and sharp voice as you say suddenly *or does it make you feel nervous and upset?* Emphasize that the details of the scene and the choice of colors cause you to feel peaceful. The cause is the scene, and the effect is the peaceful mood. Provide students with an opportunity to create a mood. Give them drawing paper and colored pencils. Encourage students to use music to create a mood with lines and colors. Play a short selection of peaceful music, followed by a short selection of louder, harsher music. Invite students to share their visual representations with each other, stating a cause-and-effect relationship, if capable.

II. READ THE LITERATURE

VOCABULARY
husking
landlord
keg
oblige
rascals
sprawled

Vocabulary

Print the vocabulary words on the chalkboard. Point to each word while saying them. Form six cooperative groups. Assign each group a word. Tell students on which page their word is located in the selection, and provide each group with a dictionary. Direct them to look in the dictionary for a definition, and then to check its context in the story. As the groups are working, circulate to demonstrate meaning of individual words, if necessary. When groups have decided upon a definition, tell them to practice a group pantomime to present to the other groups. Gather students, and allow each group to present its vocabulary word. Groups start out by stating the word and then proceed to act it out. Elicit verbal responses from the audience to check for understanding.

Evaluate Prior Knowledge

CONCEPT
another time and place

Make three posters on construction paper, labeling them: disagreement, fight/war, and destruction. Illustrate the posters with appropriate drawings or photographs. Explain that things happen in a certain order because one thing causes something else to happen. Arrange the posters on the chalk ledge in random order. Ask students to raise their hands if they know the names of any wars or battles that the United States has been involved in. Tell them that you are going to talk about the order of certain events in history. While you describe the events, challenge students to look carefully at the pictures to decide in which order they should be placed. Say: *Wars usually begin when people disagree about something. Instead of talking through their problems, people may decide to fight. When the colonists in the United States became angry with England, they decided to fight back. The colonists went to war against the British. Because of the fighting, one side lost too many soldiers and too much damage was done to the land. This caused the war to come to an end.* Invite volunteers to come to the chalk ledge and place the pictures in order. Encourage students to describe all the cause-and-effect relationships you just mentioned. Challenge them to discuss other historical causes and effects they know.

Develop Oral Language

Invite students to analyze the cause and effects of war. Elicit ideas on ways in which wars can be avoided.

nonverbal prompt for active participation

- Preproduction: *Point to the picture that shows what happens because people can't get along.*

one- or two-word response prompt

- Early production: *What can cause a fight or a war?*

prompt for short answers to higher-level thinking skills

- Speech emergence: *If you were old enough at the time of this war, would you have decided to go fight? What do you think might have happened if you had fought?*

prompt for detailed answers to higher-level thinking skills

- Intermediate fluency: *How could wars be avoided? Why do you think people decide to fight? What are some of the effects of a war?*

Guided Instruction

Preview and Predict

Tell students that you are going to discuss what they think the selection will be about, based on the illustrations. Explain that this is a play. As they look at the pictures, tell students to find a picture of the setting, or where the story takes place. Ask if they think the story is happening now or if it takes place long ago. Say: *Point to something in the picture that makes you believe that this story is not happening now. Does anything in the illustrations make you think this story is real or make-believe? Could it be both? Can you tell by looking at the illustrations what the problem in the story will be? If you can, point to it. Who do you think the title character might be? Point to him. How do you think the story might end, happily or not?*

GRAPHIC ORGANIZER
Blackline Master 105

Objectives
- To review cause and effect
- To work cooperatively

Materials

One copy of Blackline Master 105 per student; pencils

Review with students cause-and-effect relationships. Model this concept by turning off the lights (effect) and asking students to identify what caused this to happen. (flipping the light switch) Go over the chart with students. Point to the left column, cause, and explain that this is why something happens—point to the right side, effect, and say that this is what happens. Instruct students to complete the chart as they read the story. Begin the chart for them by explaining some of the history behind the story. Tell them that the colonists became very angry (use facial expressions) because England made them pay a lot of money for things. (Use gestures to show someone paying for something.) Complete the first part of the chart with them, using this information. Allow students to work together to complete the chart during the reading, where fluent readers support those needing assistance.

III. BUILD SKILLS

Comprehension

REVIEW CAUSE AND EFFECT
Blackline Master 106

Objectives
• To identify cause-and-effect relationships
• To practice following directions

Materials
One copy of Blackline Master 106 per student; colored pencils

Tell students to look at the boxes. Explain that the boxes on the left show an effect, or what happened, and the boxes on the right tell the cause, or why it happened. Read the words under the first box, pretending to be angry. Say: *Dame Van Winkle is angry. Do you know why she is angry?* Read the three possible answers, and ask students to tell which is the cause of Dame Van Winkle's anger. Instruct students to connect this cause box with the effect. Have students complete the page.

INFORMAL ASSESSMENT

Remind students that Judy says, *"Hear the thunder!"* Act this out for students as they follow along in the text. Ask a volunteer to say why Judy thought she heard thunder.

Comprehension

REVIEW DRAW CONCLUSIONS
Blackline Master 107

Objectives
• To practice drawing conclusions
• To develop understanding of character traits

Materials
One copy of Blackline Master 107 per student; colored pencils or crayons

Tell students to think about the character Rip Van Winkle. Point to the first picture, and ask a volunteer to explain what is happening. Elicit a yes or no response by asking: *Is this something that Rip would do?* If students have agreed on a response of yes, tell them to color the picture. If the response is no, tell them to leave the picture uncolored. Have students study each pair of pictures and color the one that shows something Rip Van Winkle would do.

INFORMAL ASSESSMENT

Read and act out the following passage from the story: *Rip (groaning): Ouch, my back! It's so stiff. And my legs—just like pokers.* Ask students why Rip might have said this.

Vocabulary Strategy

REVIEW SYNONYMS AND ANTONYMS
Blackline Master 108

Objectives
• Review recognition of synonyms and antonyms
• To practice following directions

Materials
One copy of Blackline Master 108 per student; colored pencils; scissors; paste or glue

Remind students that synonyms are words that have the same meaning. Model, using the words *happy/glad*. Say each word, pointing to your face as you smile. Tell them that antonyms are opposites. Use the example of *happy/sad*, using facial expressions. Tell them that the words in the triangles (point) are antonyms and the words in the circles (point) are synonyms. Focus on the antonyms first. Read the first word on the chart, *hot,* and fan yourself to aid understanding. Read the words in the triangles, using actions if possible. Have students decide which word means the opposite of hot. Instruct students to cut out the triangles and circles. Tell them to paste the triangles next to the words with opposite meanings and paste the circles next to the words with the same meanings.

INFORMAL ASSESSMENT

Direct students to the beginning of Scene 1. Print the word *right* on the chalkboard, say it, and hold out your right hand to clarify meaning. Ask students to name the antonym of this word.

Review Cause and Effect

Cause   **Effect**

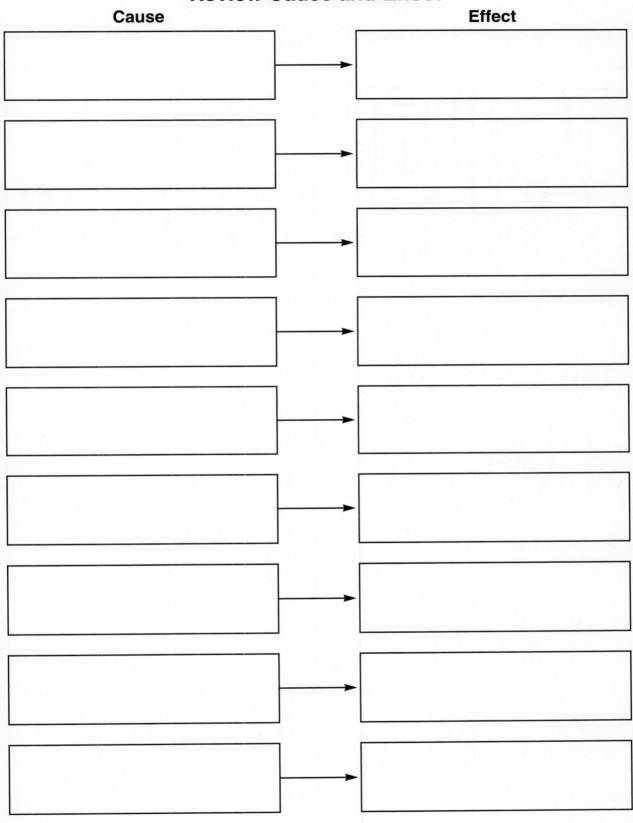

Ninepin Cause and Effect

1. Draw a line connecting each effect to its cause.

Dame Van Winkle is angry

…because he slept for twenty years.

Rip takes a nap

…because Rip didn't do his chores.

Rip wakes looking old and frail

…because the drink made him sleepy.

Which Would Rip Choose?

1. Look at the three pairs of pictures. **2.** Color the pictures that best show what Rip would most likely do in each situation. **3.** Discuss with a partner why you think so.

Synonyms and Antonyms

1. Cut out the triangles and circles at the bottom of the page. **2.** Paste the triangles next to a word that means the opposite. **3.** Paste the circle next to a word that means the same.

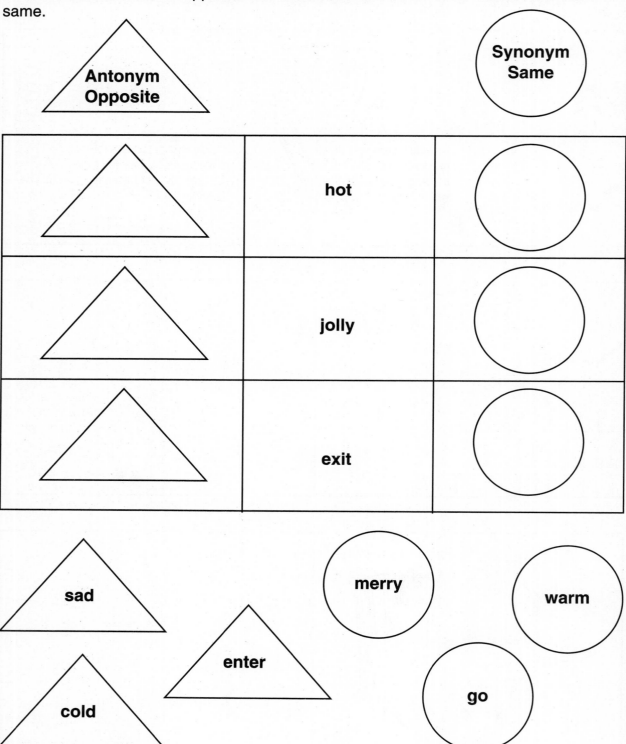

SEA MAIDENS OF JAPAN pp. 674A–697P

Written by Lili Bell Illustrated by Eric McGonigle Brammer

BUILD BACKGROUND FOR LANGUAGE SUPPORT

I. FOCUS ON READING

Focus on Skills

Develop Visual Literacy

OBJECTIVE: Review sequence of events

TPR

Have students turn to page 674. Encourage class to look closely at the details in the picture. Ask the class to point to and name things they recognize. Explain to them that it shows women working. Tell them that it was carved in wood and is called a wood-cut. Say: *When you do a job or make a craft, things need to be done in a certain order.* Provide an example of a sequence of events. Explain that painters follow a sequence of events to paint a house. First they prepare the house by washing everything and sanding the areas that need it. They might use tape or other materials to protect areas where they don't want the paint to be. Next they paint a first coat and let the paint dry. Then they will paint a second coat, if necessary. Finally the painters clean up. Have students look back at the picture. Ask: *What do you think the women do first? What do you think they do next? What is the last thing you think they do? What do you think the words written in Japanese on the scroll at the top say?*

Invite students to act out the sequence of events they think the women follow.

II. READ THE LITERATURE

Vocabulary

VOCABULARY
disgrace
cove
host
driftwood
flail
sizzle

Print the vocabulary words on pieces of paper the size of an index card. Say each word, and hold it up for all students to see. Give a brief description of each by putting them in context clues, using modeling and gestures when possible. Prepare sentence strips using the sentences from the selection that contain the vocabulary words. Omit the vocabulary words from the sentences. Pantomime the meaning of the first word as you say it aloud. Read the sentences. Select a volunteer to place the vocabulary card next to the sentence in which it belongs. Reread the sentence using the selected vocabulary word. Have students listen for meaning. If the class agrees, direct them to respond *yes*. If students disagree, they are to respond *no* and suggest the appropriate word. Some examples of context clues:

disgrace – Many cultures feel it is a *disgrace* to fail.

sizzle – Eggs *sizzle* in the frying pan.

flail – Fish *flail* when taken out of water.

driftwood – Wood found on or near water is called *driftwood*.

host – When I invite people to my home, I try to be a good *host*.

cove – If it starts to rain while near the sea you can always go to a *cove* for shelter.

CONCEPT
unusual occupations

Print the word *occupation* on the chalkboard. Tell students that an occupation is a job. Say: *My occupation is a teacher. I teach for my job. Some occupations are unusual. Being a teacher is not unusual, because there are teachers everywhere in the world.* Ask students to share any unusual occupations with which they are familiar. As language proficient students share ideas, pantomime or model occupations to help those students needing additional support. Find pictures of a few unusual occupations, such as lobster fishers, piano tuner, billboard painter. Provide students with drawing paper, and ask them to draw an occupation or job that they think is unusual. Allow students to share their drawings one by one and tell or pantomime the function of the occupation.

Develop Oral Language

nonverbal prompt for active participation

• Preproduction: *Show me* (point to self) *which occupation in the pictures you think is the most unusual. Have you ever seen anyone who does this* (point to a picture)?

one- or two-word response prompt

• Early production: *What is the name of the unusual occupation you chose? Have you ever met someone with that occupation?*

prompt for short answers to higher-level thinking skills

• Speech emergence: *What occupation would you like to learn more about? Do you know what you'd like to do when you're older?*

prompt for detailed answers to higher-level thinking skills

• Intermediate fluency: *The character in the story we'll be reading has an unusual occupation. What makes an occupation unusual? Can you tell me what you know about an unusual occupation?*

Guided Instruction

Preview and Predict

Have students quickly flip through the pages in the story. Ask the class to predict what the story might be about. Then have students look at the title picture. Ask them to predict who the main character is. Ask: *What is the girl holding in her hand? Look at the picture on page 678. What do you think those people are doing in the water? On the next page, why do you think the woman is tying a rope around the little girl's waist? Look at the next few pages. What do you see coming out of the water? What do you think will happen once they are on land? Look at the large illustration of the turtle. What do you think is happening? Do you know where turtles lay their eggs?*

GRAPHIC ORGANIZER
Blackline Master 109

Objectives
• To develop an understanding of sequence of events
• To practice following directions

Materials

One copy of Blackline Master 109 per student; pencils

Remind students that noticing the sequence of events, or order in which things happen in a story, aids comprehension. Print the following words on the chalkboard: *first, then, next, before, after, finally, last.* Explain to students that as they read the story, they will complete the chart with the important things that happen in the story. Tell them that the events need to be listed in a special way to show in what order they happened. Help them fill in the first box with the following event: *Okaasan teaches Kiyomi to dive along the shallow reefs.* Pantomime for students how to dive. Allow students to complete the boxes in the chart with drawings as well as short-word responses.

Students might also use the chart to show how turtles are born. They can start with the adult turtles coming in from the ocean and end with the baby turtles swimming away in the ocean.

III. BUILD SKILLS

Comprehension

REVIEW SEQUENCE OF EVENTS
Blackline Master 110

Objectives
• To understand sequence of events
• To work cooperatively

Materials
One copy of Blackline Master 110 per student; colored pencils or crayons; scissors; paste or glue; construction paper

Tell students to color the pictures and then cut them out. Look at each picture one at a time, and ask students to describe what is happening. Paraphrase responses, and list them on the chalkboard. Have students label each picture with the appropriate caption. Instruct students to place the pictures in order on their desks to show how Kiyomi learned to dive. After they have checked to make sure that the pictures are in the correct sequence, tell students to paste them on construction paper. Have students label their work "How Kiyomi Learned to Dive." Allow students to take turns telling the events to each other.

INFORMAL ASSESSMENT

On the chalkboard, print the following sentence from the story: *After two full moons pass, I see a nest hatch on the star cove.* Ask students to identify which event happens first—the nest hatching or the moons passing.

Comprehension

REVIEW CAUSE AND EFFECT
Blackline Master 111

Objectives
• To reinforce understanding of cause and effect relationships
• To participate in a cooperative learning exercise

Materials
One copy of Blackline Master 111 per student; scissors; glue or paste

Have students look at the pictures on the page. Read the caption for each picture, and use body language and gestures when possible to aid comprehension. Read the words in the boxes at the bottom of the page. Explain that these are the causes of the events in the pictures above. As necessary, review the idea of cause and effect. Instruct students to cut out the cause boxes and paste them in the correct effect boxes. Students may color the pictures.

INFORMAL ASSESSMENT

Print and read aloud the following passage: *"Kiyomi, when you're older and follow our tradition, ... you will not have the rope attached to your waist. You must find your own way without me." ... Hearing this, my stomach flutters.* Ask students to name the cause and effect in this situation.

Vocabulary Strategy

REVIEW CONTEXT CLUES
Blackline Master 112

Objectives
• To understand vocabulary from the story
• To practice following directions

Materials
One copy of Blackline Master 112 per student; pencils

Read the words at the top of the page together, using explanations and body language to demonstrate meaning. Read each sentence in the letter with students. Model the first one by selecting the correct vocabulary term and writing it in the blank. Pair students requiring language support with able readers. Instruct students to complete the letter, placing the appropriate word in each sentence. Encourage students to read their completed letters aloud to check for accuracy.

INFORMAL ASSESSMENT

Direct students' attention to page 683. Print the word hush on the chalkboard, and then write the following sentence from the story: *I cup my hand over my mouth to hush my giggling* … Read the sentence, and ask a volunteer to pantomime or define the word.

Sequence of Events

Learning to Dive

1. Write a word or words to describe each picture below. **2.** Cut out the pictures. **3.** Put them in order to show what happened.

_____   _____

_____   _____

Cause and Effect Match

1. Look at each picture below. 2. Read the sentence in each picture. 3. Find the cause of each, cut it out, and paste it in the box below the picture.

Kiyomi puts the baby turtle into the water

Kiyomi sits on the edge of the boat while the others are in the water

Kiyomi is underwater holding on to the sea turtle

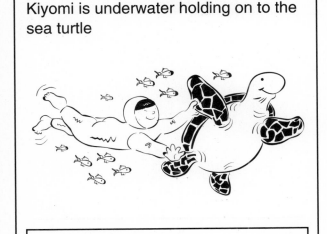

Kiyomi sits around the fire with the other ama's

...because the baby turtle was lost.

...because Kiyomi is now a brave ama.

...because the sea turtle comes to Kiyomi's boat.

...because Kiyomi is afraid of the deep water.

Kiyami's Letter

1. Use the words above to fill in the blanks in Kiyami's letter.

| abalone | driftwood | cove | disgrace | turtles | ama |

Dear Sisters,

I am learning to dive with the _____. I work hard and

do not want to _____ Mother. I watch Mother dive

from the shore of the special _____. Soon I will hunt

for _____ with the others. Today I found a piece of

_____ in the sand. Tonight, Mother and I are going to

watch for sea _____. I hope you are well.

Love,

Kiyomi

THE SILENT LOBBY pp. 698A–717P

Written by Mildred Pitts Walter Illustrated by Gil Ashby

BUILD BACKGROUND FOR LANGUAGE SUPPORT

I. FOCUS ON READING

Focus on Skills

Develop Visual Literacy

OBJECTIVE: Review judgments and decisions

TPR

Tell students that when you make judgments and decisions, it is important to think about each detail that leads you to a decision. Provide an example by saying: *The other morning, when I woke up, it seemed darker than usual. I looked out the window and saw a dark sky. I turned on the news and listened to the weather. There was a good chance of rain. I decided to wear a raincoat and bring my umbrella.* Encourage students to identify the details and the decision in this scenario. Then have students look at the painting carefully, focusing on all the details. Ask students to respond with *yes* or *no*, short one- or two-word responses, or by pointing. Say: *Do you see anything that might show us that Dr. Martin Luther King, Jr. was a religious man? Do you see a church window? The people marching with the flags are having a parade. Usually parades honor people. Why do you think they are having a parade? Who do you think they are honoring? What does this painting tell you about Martin Luther King, Jr.?*

II. READ THE LITERATURE

Vocabulary

VOCABULARY
register
interpret
pelted
soothing
persuade
shabby

Print the vocabulary words on the chalkboard. Next to each word, provide the page from the text on which each word can be found. Tell students to find the word. Ask a volunteer to read the sentence containing the word. After the word is read in context, say: *Let's see if we can figure out the meaning. I am going to put two choices on the chalkboard. I am going to select a volunteer to circle the best definition.* Print the following choices for each vocabulary word. Use body movement and gestures when possible to clarify meaning.

register—to jump/to have one's name put on a list

interpret—to explain the meaning of/to draw

pelted—struck over and over with small hard things/sewn on a machine

soothing—very cold/quiet or calming

persuade—to urge or convince/to put to sleep

shabby—made of wood/worn-out and faded

To check comprehension, pose the following questions:

- *Would you be <u>pelted</u> with air or with drops of hail?*
- *Would you <u>interpret</u> a poem or an ice cream cone?*
- *Would you <u>register</u> to vote or to eat dinner at home?*
- *Would a nice, warm bath or a loud song be <u>soothing</u>?*
- *Would you <u>persuade</u> your mother or your younger sister to take you to the movies?*
- *Would your new shirt or old jeans be <u>shabby</u>?*

Evaluate Prior Knowledge

CONCEPT
voting

Tell students that voting involves making a decision about something. Explain that you are going to give students a decision to make, and that they should think carefully about the two choices they will be given. Explain that the day a vote is made is called election day. Plan a class election. Decide upon an issue for which there are two choices. A possibility might be the type of recess activity students want. Two choices could be playing a sport in the gym or outside or staying in the classroom to play board games or similar group games. Prepare ballots with the two choices. Demonstrate for students how to mark their choice. Collect the ballots and explain how votes are tallied. Announce the election results.

Develop Oral Language

nonverbal prompt for active participation

- Preproduction: *Show me your ballot. Point to the two choices.*

one- or two-word response prompt

- Early production: *Which activity choice do you like best? How will you mark your ballot?*

prompt for short answers to higher-level thinking skills

- Speech emergence: *Was it easy or difficult to make your decision? Why?*

prompt for detailed answers to higher-level thinking skills

- Intermediate fluency: *Why did you vote for the activity you chose? What are some different kinds of elections you know about? Can you tell us how people vote in elections?*

Guided Instruction

Preview and Predict

Tell students to concentrate on the illustrations as you ask the following questions. Reassure them that they are not expected to know the correct answer. Say: *Look at the boy in the first illustration. Where do you think he is? Where do you suppose he may be going? What color skin do the characters have? Do you think it will make a difference in the story? Point to the picture of the broken-down bus. What might have happened to the bus? Has this ever happened to you?* Direct attention to the picture of the people from Mississippi meeting Congressman Hawkins. Say: *What does it look like the people are doing here? What could they be looking at? Point to the man with white skin. How does his face look? Does he look friendly or not? Look at the illustration of the big meeting. Point to the flag. Where do you think these people are? Why are they there? What color skin do they have? Look at the people on the next page. Where are they? What are they watching? Look at the last photo. How is that different from the other illustrations?*

GRAPHIC ORGANIZER
Blackline Master 113

Objectives

- To develop recognition and understanding of judgments and decisions
- To work cooperatively
- To practice following directions

Materials

One copy of Blackline Master 113 per student; pencils

Print the word *judgments* on the chalkboard while students find it on their charts. Say: *A judgment is the way someone feels or thinks about something.* Print *decisions* on the board, and say: *After a character makes a judgment about something, he or she makes a decision, or decides what to do.* Model this idea for students prior to reading. One possibility might be the following: Tell students to suppose that it's raining out and there is thunder and lightning. Pantomime as necessary. Explain that you have a soccer game today (you might show kicking a soccer ball and running). Point out the window, and say: *There's rain, thunder, and lightning outside. It would not be safe to play outside. We will not have the soccer game.* Explain that as students read the story, they will complete the chart in the same way, writing the judgments on the left and the decisions on the right.

Students can also use the chart to record two judgments and decisions from the story. Below each decision from the story, they should state whether they agree or disagree with it. Encourage students to include in the chart anything they would do differently.

III. BUILD SKILLS

Comprehension

REVIEW JUDGMENTS AND DECISIONS
Blackline Master 114

Objectives
- To review recognizing judgments and decisions
- To practice following directions

Materials
One copy of Blackline Master 114 per student; pencils

Remind students that when people vote, they make a decision about an issue. Explain that students will make some decisions about issues by voting *yes* or *no* (nod and shake your head). Tell students to listen carefully to each question you ask about school and to look at the pictures to help them understand each question. If they think the idea is a good one, instruct students to mark the *yes* box with an X. If they disagree, show how to mark the *no* box. Use gestures and pantomime as much as possible when reading each item.

INFORMAL ASSESSMENT

Remind students that in the story, Papa is upset because people with black skin are not allowed to vote. Ask them to pretend they are Papa and say if they feel this law is fair or not.

Comprehension

REVIEW DRAW CONCLUSIONS
Blackline Master 115

Objectives
- To review drawing conclusions
- To practice following directions

Materials
One copy of Blackline Master 115 per student; pencils

Brainstorm with students a list of adjectives that describe emotion. Write the words on the chalkboard. Use facial expressions to model each emotion: lonely, sad, happy, mad, upset, (add student-generated ideas). Point to the first picture, and discuss with students what is happening. Point to each word on the chalkboard, using facial expressions to remind them of meaning. Instruct students to choose one or two words that describe the picture. Have students write one or two words for the remaining pictures.

INFORMAL ASSESSMENT

Direct attention to the first illustration—the boy in the bus window. Ask students to choose a word from the chalkboard that describes how the boy in the picture might feel.

Vocabulary Strategy

REVIEW SYNONYMS AND ANTONYMS
Blackline Master 116

Objectives
- To recognize synonyms and antonyms
- To practice following directions

Materials
One copy of Blackline Master 116 per student; pencils

Go over the page with students. Begin by reviewing that synonyms are words that have the same meaning and antonyms are opposites. Have students point to the bold words and repeat after you. Say each word in the right column, modeling meaning as necessary. Instruct students to say *yes* if the word has similar meaning to the bold word in that row. When students decide on a synonym, tell them to circle their choice. Ask students to go back through the word list and check that the other word choices have opposite meanings. Direct students to draw a line underneath each antonym. Invite students to check charts with each other for accuracy.

INFORMAL ASSESSMENT

Print the word *laughing* on the chalkboard. Explain that this word appears in the story. Model the act of laughing. Ask a volunteer to suggest a word that means the same as laughing (such as giggle) and a word that means the opposite (such as crying).

Judgments and Decisions

Judgments	Decisions

Decide Your Vote

1. Write an X in the box for the answer you agree with. 2. Tally the class votes.

Question 1: Should students be allowed to bring pets to this school?

☐ Yes   ☐ No

Question 2: Should students in school have recess?

☐ Yes   ☐ No

Question 3: Should students have ice cream for lunch?

☐ Yes   ☐ No

Question 4: Should students have homework?

☐ Yes   ☐ No

What Do You See?

1. Look at the pictures. **2.** Write one or two words to describe each picture.

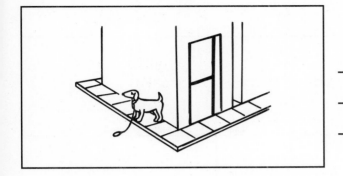

_____

_____

_____

_____

_____

_____

_____

_____

_____

_____

_____

_____

Synonyms and Antonyms

1. Read each bold word in the left column of the chart below. **2.** Draw a circle around the word in the column on the right that is its synonym (same). **3.** Underline the word in the column on the right that is its antonym (opposite).

scared	afraid	calm
for	against	with
shabby	worn	fancy
soothing	calming	exciting
persuade	encourage	discourage
silent	quiet	loud

AMON ALERT! pp. 718A–727P

BUILD BACKGROUND FOR LANGUAGE SUPPORT

I. FOCUS ON READING
Focus on Skills

Develop Visual Literacy

OBJECTIVE: Review sequence of events

Review with students that sequencing involves understanding that things happen in a certain order. Ask them to look at the photograph *Rock and Flower* on page 718 and identify the flower by pointing to it. Have students acknowledge whether or not they have flowers near their homes or have had experience growing them. Say: *What is the name of the small thing we plant to grow a flower? What does it look like? Show or tell me where seeds are planted. What is needed for a seed to grow?* Focus students' attention back onto the photograph. Say: *Show me the flower in the picture. Show me where the seed for this flower must have been planted. What do you think happened after the seed was planted? Can you imagine how this flower grew?*

TPR

Invite students to pantomime the growth of a flower. Model, crouching in a ball on the floor, then slowly standing up, and finally spreading your arms wide as if reaching up for the sun.

II. READ THE LITERATURE

Vocabulary

VOCABULARY

lush
tropical
variety
wonderland
confirmed
isolated

Print the vocabulary words on index cards. Gather students close to you so they can see the words clearly. Say each word, and state its meaning, using pantomime and expression. Then read the sentences from Teaching Chart 176. If available, accompany this activity with a picture of a rainforest to help students visualize the words as well. If class has been on a trip to a zoo or botanical garden with a rain forest section, help class recall the trip: *lush*—lots of growth, full; *tropical*—hot, wet climate; *variety*—many kinds; *wonderland*—a wonderful, magical place; *confirmed*—proven true; *isolated*—alone. On the back of each word card, prepare a clue for a different vocabulary word. Spread the cards on a table, desk, or floor, with the vocabulary words face-up. The first player selects a card and reads the clue on the back. The next player points to the vocabulary word that fits the clue. When everyone agrees that this is correct, that player picks up the card and reads the next clue on the back. The last card should lead back to the vocabulary word on the card the first player picked. Play the game enough times for all students to get a turn. This activity would follow along nicely with the concept of sequence of events and cycles.

Evaluate Prior Knowledge

CONCEPT
sequence of events

Remind students that sequencing means "putting things in order." Explain that understanding the sequence or order in which things happen in a story helps us to understand and better remember the story. Practice sequencing activities with students. Use familiar activities, such as getting ready for school in the morning. Act out the following actions, and say what you're doing: *First I wake up. Then I get dressed. Next I brush my teeth and fix my hair. Then I have breakfast and make my lunch for school. Finally I drive to school.* Invite a volunteer to mirror the activity. Ask students to decide if that person remembered each step in the correct sequence. Repeat, using a different familiar routine, such as making a sandwich. Invite volunteers to model and narrate an activity in sequence.

Develop Oral Language

nonverbal prompt for active participation

- Preproduction: *Show me* (point to self) *the first thing you do when you wake up in the morning. Do you always do this?*

one- or two-word response prompt

- Early production: *What is one thing I do in the morning that you also do? What is one thing you do that I didn't say?*

prompt for short answers to higher-level thinking skills

- Speech emergence: *Do you make your own lunch? What is the first thing you do when you make your lunch? What is the first thing someone else does, if you don't make your lunch?*

prompt for detailed answers to higher-level thinking skills

- Intermediate fluency: *Can you tell me what steps you follow to get ready for bed at night?*

Guided Instruction

Preview and Predict

Tell students to look carefully at the illustrations in *Amazon Alert!* Remind them that this is a non-fiction selection. Explain that the Amazon is a rainforest, and show its location on the map in the article. Have students point to the location on the map. Say: *Look at the title photograph. Point to the trees. Do they look like the trees you are used to seeing? What has happened to them? How did this happen? Why do you suppose the trees look this way? Do you see animals living here? Do you see water? Look at the picture of the birds. Do you know what kind of birds they are? Have you seen these types of birds flying near your house? Where do you think they live? Can you show me on the title photograph? A graph tells information. Point to the largest bar on the graph. What do you think that shows? Look at the photograph of the woman. Who do you think she is? What do you think we will learn about her?*

GRAPHIC ORGANIZER
Blackline Master 117

Objectives
- To recognize and record sequence of events
- To practice following directions

Materials
One copy of Blackline Master 117 per student; pencils

Explain to students that this chart will be used to tell the order of what happens. Pair students needing language support with more fluent speakers. Read the first paragraph and the first sentence of the second paragraph with students. Tell students that they will record the sequence of events that has caused the shrinking of the Amazon rainforest. Help students understand that the destruction is caused by cutting down trees. Act out cutting down a tree to provide a visual clue. Allow students to record information using one or two words if necessary. Encourage them to use the dates mentioned in the article to help sequence the events.